# Buses and Trams
# of Scotland and Ireland
# 1950s-1970s

# Buses and Trams of Scotland and Ireland 1950s-1970s

## The operators and their vehicles

## Part 1: Aberdeen, Dundee and Edinburgh

### Henry Conn

**SLP**

**Silver Link Publishing Ltd**

First published in 2012

British Library Cataloguing in Publication Data

A catalogue record for this book is available from the British Library.

ISBN 978 1 85794 400 6

*Title page:* **Towards the end of 1934 the prototype of a new standard design of Edinburgh tram, No 69, was completed in Shrubhill, and the type went into production immediately, a total of 26 being produced in 1935. No 165 entered service in 1935 and is seen here in Princes Street at just** **after 4 o'clock in the afternoon on 3 July 1956. The bus on the other side of the road is one of the batch of 100 Metro-Cammell-bodied Leyland PD2/20s delivered during 1955 for tram replacement services.** *David Clarke*

Silver Link Publishing Ltd
The Trundle
Ringstead Road
Great Addington
Kettering
Northants NN14 4BW

Tel/Fax: 01536 330588
email: sales@nostalgiacollection.com
Website: www.nostalgiacollection.com

Printed and bound in the Czech Republic

All photographs not otherwise credited were taken by the author or are from his collection. Those labelled 'transporttreasury.co.uk' are obtainable from Transport Treasury.

## Acknowledgements

**M**any of the photographs within this book have come from my collection, but my most sincere thanks go to David Clarke for allowing continued and much-appreciated access to his wonderful collection of negatives and slides. David's portraits of the trams of Aberdeen, Dundee and Edinburgh from the early 1950s through to the early 1960s are rare and exceptional. Many thanks also to Geof Gould and Phil Sposito, and to Transport Treasury for safely archiving many of my negatives and slides.

The PSV publications of all the operators illustrated, and many early issues of *Buses Illustrated*, were vital sources of information for this book.

# Contents

This fine view of Aberdeen tram No 29 was taken on the single-track terminal stub at Bridge of Don on 10 July 1956. The area behind the tram was at times used for visiting circuses and remained underdeveloped for a few years after the trams stopped in 1958.

The area to the left became the Seaton flats in 1966, and the volume of traffic has changed! The shop in the background, Pirie's, was closed by the time this view was taken, and the building was subsequently demolished. *David Clarke*

# Introduction

This is the first of three volumes that will cover operators in Scotland and Ireland. This one is dedicated to the Corporation fleets of Aberdeen, Dundee and Edinburgh, and includes large selections of views of trams from all three operators from the camera of David Clarke in the mid-1950s.

Aberdeen is my home town and my most vivid memory of the trams is travelling in the streamliners from Union Street to Bridge of Dee, then transferring to a bus for the onward journey to Garthdee to visit my grandmother. The streamliners were in my opinion the most classic of tram cars and are extensively covered in this volume, including colour views at Bridge of Don, Bridge of Dee and Hazlehead. It was a sad day when the last trams were replaced by a fleet of AEC Regent Vs, and the journey to Garthdee was never the same again.

The tram replacement fleet from 1954 was a mixture of Daimler CVG6s and AEC Regent Vs, and among the purchases were five Crossley-bodied AEC Regent Vs, Nos 205 to 209, my favourite Aberdeen buses. The last Regents, which were the first Alexander-bodied buses for the fleet, arrived in 1959.

From 1960 until 1965 Aberdeen Corporation purchased Daimler CVG6s, the vast majority being bodied by Alexander. The 1965 CVG6s were Scotland's last front-engined Daimlers, and were among the last rear-entrance buses to enter service in Scotland. Aberdeen Corporation rebuilt a number of the 1963 CVG6s to forward entrances for one-person operation, but they were not successful. From 1966 new double-deckers were a mixture of Daimler Fleetlines and Leyland Atlanteans.

The single-deck fleet was comprised of Leyland Tiger Cubs, AEC Swifts and AEC Reliances with Alexander bodywork. During 1971, however, the Corporation unusually purchased three Roe-bodied AEC Reliances from Leeds, and after successful trials three Leyland Nationals were purchased, the first for a major Scottish operator until 1975.

The main tram routes in Dundee were to Ninewells, Blackness, Maryfield, Lochee and Downfield, and the system is extensively covered in this volume with colour and black and white views taken by David Clarke in April 1955 and July 1956. In November 1955, as an experiment, the Blackness to Downfield tram route was withdrawn and replace by a fleet of Metro-Cammell-bodied Daimler CVG6s. Within a year all the remaining tram routes had been replaced by buses.

During 1955 and 1956 Dundee Corporation purchased from London Transport 10 STLs and 30 Craven-bodied RTs for tram replacement. For the next few years purchases were solely of Daimler CVG6s, most of which were bodied by Metro-Cammell, although the last batch in 1960 had Alexander bodywork. The first rear-engined double-deck buses with Alexander bodywork arrived in 1964.

Interesting purchases in 1975 were the first Leylands since 1931, comprising 15 former Edinburgh Leyland PD2s with Metro-Cammell bodywork. The last AEC double-deckers were withdrawn by 1975, but Dundee had a sizeable fleet of Reliances and Swifts. From 1971 to 1972 the Corporation also purchased 25 single-deck Fleetlines, but they were not the best buy and were extensively rebuilt with reduced seating capacity to reduce flexing of the chassis.

The Edinburgh electric tram system at

ts peak totalled 47½ miles, and even by 1952 there was still an extensive system of 28 routes, the majority of which are captured by the camera of David Clarke in the period between April 1953 and July 1956. Just a few months later, in November 1956, the trams were no more.

For tram replacement Edinburgh purchased 300 Leyland Titans with Metro-Cammell 'Orion' bodywork, noisy buses that weighed less than 6¾ tons. The last were not withdrawn until 1976. Edinburgh continued to purchase Leyland Titans, all with Alexander bodywork, and he 25 PD3s purchased in 1966 were the last new examples for a Scottish operator. From 1966 the Leyland Atlantean became Edinburgh Corporation's standard bus,

and by 1975 there were 475 in service with bodywork by Alexander, the majority fitted with panoramic windows.

Wearing a smart black and white livery, the Corporation also had a fleet of coaches providing tours of the city, which usually started at the entrance to Waverley railway station. Between 1959 and 1961 the Corporation also purchased 100 Weymann-bodied Leyland Tiger Cubs for routes with low bridges or smaller clientele. Also purchased in 1961 was No 101, which started its service life as a three-door 'pay as you enter' bus. This was not a success and the view of the bus in this volume shows it working as an airport coach from Waverley.

Enjoy the nostalgia!

Daimler Fleetline demonstrator 4559 VC was tested by Dundee Corporation in early May 1963, and this trial led to the ordering and subsequent delivery of 25 Daimler CRG6LXs with Alexander A-type bodies in 1964. The Corporation was the first recipient of the Alexander J-type bodywork, its Nos 35 to 54 being received during 1966. The third batch of J-type CRG6LXs were delivered during 1969, numbered 296 to 305 (GYJ 396G to 405G), and working variations of route 1 in the summer of 1970 are Nos 299 and, behind, 302 (GYJ 399G and GYJ 402G).

# Aberdeen Corporation

The first horse trams in Aberdeen, operated by the Aberdeen District Tramways Co, began operations on 31 August 1874, and the first lines were between Queens Cross and North Church in King Street, and from Union Street to Kittybrewster. By the end of Aberdeen District operations in 1898 there were lines to Mannofield, Rosemount, Bridge of Dee, Bridge of Don, Woodside and Bayview. On 26 August 1898 Aberdeen Corporation purchased the assets of the company and began to electrify the system. The first electric trams to Woodside began on 23 December 1899 and further extensions to the system were completed to Sea Beach in 1901 and Torry and Ferryhill in 1903.

The first bus, a Thornycroft J, began circular tours of the city on 19 July 1920 and the first bus service began on 10 January the following year between Castle Street and Footdee. Further tramway extensions were completed to Hazlehead in 1924, which included a section of line on a private right of way, and to Scatterburn in July 1938. The Pittodrie loop, for football traffic, was completed in February 1937. The first tramway abandonment was on 28 February 1931 when the Torry route ceased operations, and this was quickly followed by the Ferryhill route, which ceased on 31 May 1931.

Between 1921 and 1930 only single-deck buses were purchased, and they were either Thornycrofts or Albions. During 1930 four double-deck buses were obtained for trials, resulting in the purchase of 14 Crossley Condors, which entered service in 1931. The bus network was extended from 1926 to Garden City, Golf Links, Broomhill, Union Grove, Old Aberdeen, Hilton, Midstocket and Ashgorve Road. From 1936 until 1966, with the exception of 10 Crossley coaches in 1950, all buses purchased by the Corporation were AECs or Daimlers.

Between July and August 1940 two double-bogie and two single-bogie English Electric trams entered service, and as a result of these purchases 20 centre-entrance double-bogie trams entered service between 26 January and 30 July 1949. During the war Aberdeen lost 31 buses to the War Department, and 20 Daimler Utilities arrived between 1943 and 1945.

Trams to Mannofield ceased on 3 March 1951, and on 2 October 1954 the Rosemount circle ceased operations. This left four routes, and on 3 May 1958 the last of them, between Bridge of Dee and Bridge of Don, ran for the last time. The modern streamlined trams were offered for sale, but there were no buyers, and on the night of 12-13 May the whole of the Corporation's tram fleet was burned on the Queens Links private track. A large batch of Daimler CVG6s was purchased as tram replacements, and the last trams on the Bridges route were replaced by AEC Regent Vs.

During 1966 the Corporation purchased its first Leylands, which were single-deck PSUC1/13s equipped for one-person operation. Also in that year the first rear-engined buses entered service, Alexander-bodied Daimler CRG6LXs. From 1961 bus bodywork was by Alexander and the livery was green and cream, although the buses had grey roofs until October 1964, when this was phased out.

Between January 1947 and April 1948 Aberdeen purchased 14 former Manchester trams. They were designed by R. Stuart Pilcher, who had managed the Aberdeen system from 1906 to 1918. All the cars were extensively refurbished before entering service, and they worked most of the Union Street routes. They had lightweight bodies and were quite lively performers, although noisy. No 44 entered service in July 1948 and is seen at the Sea Beach summer terminus of route 4 in July 1954. Five of the so called 'Pilchers' were withdrawn from service in February 1955, including No 44. *transporttreasury.co.uk*

*Right:* **Seen from another 'Pilcher' in September 1950 is tram No 51, which entered service in May 1950. Route 2 ran from Castle Street, proceeding for a mile up Union Street to Holburn Junction, where it turned into Holburn Street. Following route 1 at Holburn Street, route 2 turned right onto Great Western Road and travelled some 1½ to the terminus at Mannofield. Some route 2 trams during the summer season continued to the Sea Beach terminus. Great Western Road was rather narrow in places and, with the track steadily deteriorating, route 2 became the first Aberdeen post-war tram route to close, the last tram running on 3 March 1951.** *transporttreasury. co.uk*

*Below:* **Being slightly longer than the Aberdeen standards that worked route 7 to Woodside, the 'Pilchers' were not allowed in St Nicholas Street. This is therefore a rare view of No 52 at the Woodside terminus of** route 7 in the summer of 1954. No 52 entered service in 1950 and was withdrawn from service in October 1955. Together with another two 'Pilchers', it was then used as staff rooms at King Street during garage rebuilding from 1956 until January 1958, when the trio were scrapped. *transporttreasury.co.uk*

*Above:* **Standing at the Sea Beach terminus on 11 July 1956, with a good number of passengers waiting to board, is tram No 62. Nos 62 and 63, new in 1923, were the first all-enclosed Aberdeen trams, and were built by Aberdeen Corporation utilising parts from earlier tram Nos 1 to 3 and 21 to 24. They originally had Brill 21E trucks and two 35hp BTH GE200 motors, but both were later fitted with DK108C 50hp white-metal-bearing motors. Both survived until the end of the tramway system in May 1958. Just visible in the back ground is the Beach Ballroom, built in 1926.** *David Clarke*

*Below:* **For many years the Royal Northern show was held at Hazlehead, and for the event the Corporation provided a tram every minute on route 4. At the head of a number of trams at Castle Street on 11 July 1956, and heading for the show, is No 63. The car is an Austin Cambridge A50, which was introduced in 1954 and just under 115,000 were produced until 1957. The example in this view was new in 1956, and at that time cost £720 including taxes. The British Road Services lorry on the right is a Seddon 5L, new in 1949. The tram to the right of No 63 is No 24, which entered service on the Bridges route 1 on 25 March 1949.** *David Clarke*

*Above*: Working route 4, also on 11 July 1956, is No 99. This tram was built in 1923 by Aberdeen Corporation and was an experimental high-speed car fitted with a Brill 21E truck and two 50hp BTH GE 200 motors. It was similar to Nos 62 and 63, but was slightly longer. The Brill truck was later replaced by a Peckham P35 truck, and EMB air brakes were fitted in 1940. No 99 was withdrawn from service in October 1956. The bus is No 32 (DRG 332), a Brockhouse-bodied Daimler CVG6 new to the Corporation in 1951. To the left is the Mercat Cross, designed by John Montgomery and built in 1686. The opened-arched hexagonal structure is 21 feet in diameter and 18 feet high, and includes medallions illustrating Scottish monarchs from James I to James VII. *David Clarke*

*Left:* On Union Street on 10 July 1956, about to cross the junction of Union Terrace and Bridge Street, is No 100. This tram was nicknamed the 'Jubilee' car and was built by the Corporation in 1924. It was fitted with air brakes in 1928, and withdrawn in October 1956. The building in the background is the Trades Hall, erected in 1847 at a cost exceeding £7,000. The nearest car is a Riley RME, which had a 1.5-litre straight-four engine and, when first produced in 1952, cost £1,339 including taxes. The smaller car behind No 100 is an Austin A30, which, when introduced in 1952, cost £553 including taxes. *David Clarke*

bove: This is the busy junction of Union treet, King Street (right) and Castle Street, nd approaching the camera on 11 July 1956 is am No 101, built by the Corporation in 1924 nd, like No 100, withdrawn from service in ctober of that year. Aberdeen had two native anks, the Town & Country and the North of cotland, and the building on the right was he home of the latter; esigned by Archibald impson, it was built etween 1839 and 842, and is now a pub alled the Archibald impson. The building nmediately behind lo 101 is the Royal thenaeum, which vas part of the Union uilding, also designed y Archibald Simpson. Jnfortunately, in 1973 he whole building vas burned out. *David Clarke*

right: The time is 9.14 n the morning of 12 pril 1955 and the entleman appears o be late for work nd is taking a chance

running in front of No 102. This is the single-track terminus in St Nicholas Street, and in the background can be seen the first of two passing places for the trams on route 7. The first is at the junction of Correction Wynd, and the second at the junction of School Hill. The single line ran as far as Loch Street. *David Clarke*

*Above:* **Route 7 started from St Nicholas Street, just off Union Street and opposite Market Street, and travelled just under 3 miles to Woodside, which was actually Scatterburn. The best part of 2 miles from St Nicholas Street is Woodside Fountain, and dropping and picking up passengers there on 12 April 1955 is No 102. For some unknown reason, Nos 102 and 120 exchanged numbers in the early 1930s, so at the time of this view this tram was the old No 120, which had been built by the Corporation at Dee Village Works in 1927, and was withdrawn at the closure of route 7 in November 1955.** *David Clarke*

*Below:* **At the Castlegate terminus on 10 July 1956, working route 4 to Hazlehead, is No 103 which was built by the Corporation in 1925 and was in service on the last day of tram operations on 3 May 1958. The castellated building in the background is the Salvation Army Citadel, designed by James Souttar and built between 1893 and 1896. The nearest car is a Vauxhall Cresta E. Note the Corporation employee carrying a board for the greyhound racing at Bridge of Dee.** *David Clarke*

*Above:* Just short of the end of Queen's Road, route 4 to Hazlehead branched left to the terminus at the end of a reserved track. This gave access to Hazlehead Park and recreation grounds, and exiting the reserved track heading for Castle Street on 11 July 1956 is No 105. In the background is the Woodend stub, where in winter the majority of route 4 trams terminated. The Hazlehead reserved track closed in October 1956 and the main portion of route 4 to Woodend finished on 19 November. Tram No 105 was built by Aberdeen Corporation in 1925 and was still on fleet strength on the last day of operations in May 1958. The other tram is No 135, a Brush-built car that entered service on 28 October 1929. *David Clarke*

*Right:* **During 1925** Aberdeen took delivery of Nos 107 to 115, which were built by Brush and when new had Peckham P35 trucks and two BTH GE200 35hp motors. Nos 107, 108 and 111 to 115 were fitted with DK motors in 1928, but 109 and 110 retained their original motors and worked on the Woodside route until their withdrawal in 1954. This is No 113 on the Beach reserved track on 10 July 1956 working route 4 but showing Depot on the cloth. The tram journey from Castle Street to Sea Beach was less than a mile long and descended through the run-down area of Justice Street, into Constitution Street, over a railway bridge and onto a quarter-mile-long reserved track that curved to the left to a terminal stub at the Beach Ballroom. *David Clarke*

This wonderful view of Union Street was taken in the summer of 1954 and the nearest tram is No 107, which, with No 108, was in service on the last day of the trams. One of the most striking features on Union Street is the Façade, designed by John Smith in 1830, which is made up of 12 Doric columns with an arched gateway. Behind the Façade is the Kirkyard of St Nicholas, where many of the city's noted

*Above:* **Passing Broad Street and the Town House at 1.00pm on 10 July 1956 on a shortened route 1 to School Road is No 115. Built by Brush in 1925, Nos 107 to 115 were 30ft 2in long and 7 feet wide, the bodies were teak, and the seats were originally covered in blue leather cloth. The smart car with white-wall tyres is a four-door Ford Prefect 100E, which had an 1172cc engine with a three-speed manual transmission, and in 1957 cost £658.** *David Clarke*

*Below:* **Ordered in March 1929 were 12 Brush-built trams, Nos 126 to 137, and they were nicknamed 'The English Cars'. The first car, No 126, was inspected by the Aberdeen Tramways Committee on 27 September 1929 and entered service on the Hazlehead route on 6 October. It is seen here at 4.00pm on 11 April 1955 heading for Castle Street along Union Street working route 4. No 126 was withdrawn in October of the following year.** *David Clarke*

*Above:* This is Castle Street on 11 July 1956 and No 126 is seen again picking up a few customers for the trip to Hazlehead. Judging by the posture of the Corporation employee, he looks as though he has a bad day at the office and is a wee bit miffed! A bottle of Wallace's Old Scotch Whisky will now set you back around £75. *David Clarke*

*Below:* Heading for Queens Cross depot at 7.43 in the evening of 10 July 1956 is No 128, which entered service on route 4 on 8 October 1929 and was withdrawn in October 1956. Queens Cross depot was opened in 1874, but as the tram routes closed it became more and more a storage depot for withdrawn cars. Trams for the Bridges route 1 were not allocated to Queens Cross from February 1957. The depot was sold to Grampian Television, and conversion to a studio began in November 1960. The car in the background is a Hillman Minx. *David Clarke*

*Above:* Working route 4 on Queens Road on the 11 July 1956, heading for town, is tram No 134, which entered service on 20 October 1929 and was initially allocated to the Queens Cross Circle. On the right is the boundary of Rubislaw Quarry, which opened in 1740. It is estimated that more than 6 million tonnes of granite were excavated from the quarry, which, at 142 metres deep and with a diameter of 120 metres, is one of the biggest man-made holes in Europe. It closed in 1971 and is now filled with water 50 metres deep. The van to the right is a Ford Thames 300E. *David Clarke*

*Below:* No 134 is seen again heading up from the Sea Beach terminus during the early evening rush-hour traffic on 10 July 1956. It will travel along Constitution Street, Park Street and Justice Street before entering Castlegate. Nos 126 to 137 were fine trams and were the first Aberdeen cars to have flush sides instead of the inward curve of the body towards the truck. Because of the extra width they were also the first to have transverse seating downstairs. Nos 132 to 137 remained available for service until the end of the system, but only 135 worked on the last day. *David Clarke*

*Above:* The tall building to the left of this view of Union Street is the Town House, work on which began in 1867. It was designed by Messrs Peddie & Kinnear of Edinburgh at an estimated cost of £69,000, but when completed the cost had soared to more than £80,000. Working route 1 to Bridge of Dee in the late afternoon of 10 July 1956 is No 135, which appeared on the final procession of Aberdeen trams on 3 May 1958. An interesting selection of cars on the left includes a Ford Zephyr Six, a Volkswagen Type 1 with two small rear windows, and an Austin A40 Somerset. The van is a Commer BF, and the bus is a Daimler CVD6. *David Clarke*

*Right:* On 12 and 24 July 1940 two new English Electric streamlined trams, Nos 138 and 139, entered service on the Bridges route 1. They had a total of 76 seats with central entrances, and, as the doors were manually operated, required two conductors until they were fitted with driver-controlled folding

doors between 1954 and 1955. Their original livery was cream with green streamlining, but after the war the lower deck colours were reversed, becoming mainly green. Both trams spent most of their time on the Bridges route with infrequent workings on the Hazlehead route. No 138 is heading north on King Street towards Bridge of Don on 11 July 1956. *David Clarke*

*Above:* This is Union Street on 10 July 1956 at the junction of Bon Accord Street, and working route 1 to Bridge of Dee is No 139. Nos 138 and 139 were 38 feet long, 7ft 2in wide and 15ft 2in high, and their unladen weight was 20 tons. The shop in the background, on the corner of Bon Accord Street, is Andrew Collie & Co, which was an up-market wines, spirits and provisions merchant. *David Clarke*

*Below:* No 139 is seen at 2.23pm on the same day, having arrived at the Bridge of Dee terminus. Towards the end of the system No 138 became rather shabby, but No 139 was still working on the Bridges route until the last few months of tram operations. From November 1948 route 1 would connect with a shuttle bus service, No 13, to the new housing development at Garthdee. *David Clarke*

*Above:* On 1 August 1940 No 140 entered service followed a few days later by No 141, built by English Electric with seating for 64. No 140 was initially allocated to route 2 to Mannofield and 141 to route 4 to Hazlehead, but 141 later joined 140 on route 2. On the closure of that route on 3 March 1951, both were allocated to route 7 to Woodside. Following the closure of that route on 26 November 1955 they appeared at times on routes 1 and 4. No 140 is seen here working route 4 to Hazlehead on Union Street on 10 July 1956. This tram was withdrawn in October 1956 and scrapped at King Street depot as an experiment to assess the costs of scrapping by the Corporation. No 141 ran very occasionally in 1956 and was withdrawn in that year, although it was still in stock in May 1958. *David Clarke*

*Right:* **Here is No 140**

again, ascending Justice Street on route 4 to Hazlehead at 4.38pm on the same day. Nos 140 and 141 were attractive cars and were delivered with a broadly similar paint scheme to Nos 138 and 139, but the livery was also reversed, with the lower panels becoming mainly green. The bus is No 164 (DRS 364), seen here with the original Northern Coachbuilders bodywork. *David Clarke*

*Above:* During 1948 Nos 140 and 141 were fitted with roller shutter platform doors, and during 1952 longitudinal seats were fitted in the lower saloon. At the tram shelter at Hazlehead, again on 10 July 1956, is No 141, which had the distinction of being the highest-numbered Aberdeen tram. *David Clarke*

were Nos 140 and 141, and seen on Great Northern Road at the junction of St Machar Drive is the latter. This view was taken on 12 April 1955, only a few months before the closure of the route on 26 November. *David Clarke*

*Right:* With the closure of the Rosemount circle routes on 2 October 1954, the tram routes that remained were the Bridges route 1, the Hazlehead/Woodend to Castle Street/Sea Beach, and route 7 from Market Street to Woodside. Route 7 was heavily used but suffered from the bottleneck at St Nicholas Street, and also could not accommodate the larger bogie trams. The newest trams used on route 7

*Above:* Virtually identical to Nos 138 and 139, 20 new trams were delivered from Pickerings of Wishaw (which built them under licence from English Electric), and they entered service between 26 January and 30 July 1949. They were numbered 19 to 38, and their EMB bogies were built by M. B. Wild & Co. All were converted to longitudinal seating in the lower saloon during 1951 and 1952, and from July 1954, starting with No 30, all had power centre doors fitted. Passing the entrance to King Street depot on the early morning of 11 July 1956 is No 19, which was the first to enter service on 26 January 1949 and was initially allocated to route 4 to Hazlehead. *David Clarke*

*Below:* Route 1, the Bridges route, was the premier tram route of the Aberdeen Corporation system and was about 4¼ miles long. Very busy at all times, running along King Street, Union Street and Holburn Street, in 1958 the route had a 4-minute basic peak-hour service. Also seen on 11 July 1956, working route 1 in King Street with St Peters Cemetery on the left, is tram No 20, which entered service on 27 January 1949 and was in service on the last day of operations in May 1958. *David Clarke*

*Above:* Turning from Union Street into Holburn Street en route to Bridge of Dee on 10 July 1956 is No 21, which entered service on 10 February 1949. The Bridges route also benefited from traffic generated by the greyhound stadium at Bridge of Dee. In certain weather conditions, particularly snow and slush, the streamliners were found to be less reliable than the older trams. For this reason, 18 older trams remained on fleet strength after 1956, as they rode quite high and were more reliable than the streamliners. The church in the background is Gilcomston South (Free) Church, notable as being one of only two sandstone buildings on Union Street.
*David Clarke*

later entered service on the Bridges route. It is seen here in Holburn Street on the same day as the previous photograph, heading for Bridge of Dee. The bus is No 221 (JRG 221), a Metro-Cammell-bodied Daimler CVG6, one of a batch of 15 that entered service in 1956 as tram replacements and cost £4,499 each.
*David Clarke*

*Right:* No 22 was first used for one day only on a Pittodrie football special on 12 February 1949, then eight days

*Above:* **Tram No 24 entered service on route 1 on 25 March 1949; just over six years later this view was taken at 11.35am on 12 April 1955 as it arrives at the Bridge of Dee terminus. The van in the background is a Ford Thames 300E, which was introduced in July 1954 and produced until April 1961, by which time nearly 197,000 had been built. The 300E van was replaced by the Ford Thames 307E, which was available from June 1961.** *David Clarke*

*Below:* **No 25 entered service on route 1 on 8 April 1949, and this view in Holburn Street was taken in mid-afternoon on 10 July 1956. The bogie trams were popular with passengers because they were warm and comfortable, with none of the draughts of the older open-platform cars. The centre entrances with access to two saloons on the lower deck and two stairs to the top deck, however, caused congestion during loading and unloading.** *David Clarke*

*Right:* **Passing the now abandoned tram lines into Union Terrace, and bound for Bridge of Dee on 1 April 1955 is No 26, which entered service on 28 April 1949. The car is a Ford Zodiac Mark I, which was an up-market version of the Zephyr launched at the London Motor Show in the autumn of 1953. It had two-tone paintwork, leather trim, a heater, windscreen washers, white-wall tyres and spotlights, and in 1955 could have been yours for £851 including taxes.** *David Clarke*

*Below:* **No 26 is seen again at the Bridge of Don terminus on the following day. The five-arch granite bridge over the River Don was originally designed by John Smith but** was later revised by Thomas Telford. The foundation stone was laid in March 1827 and it was opened in November 1830 at a total cost of £7,000. *David Clarke*

*Above:* Until 1932 all Aberdeen trams were fitted with trolley poles for current collection. From 1932 the trolley poles began to be replaced by the Fischer 'bow collector', which caused less wear on the wire and was easier to maintain. During 1936 and 1937 'bow trippers', the invention of James Wilson, chief linesman for the Corporation, were installed on the overhead contact wires at all tram termini. No 28 is at the Bridge of Dee terminus on 11 July 1956 and is about to use the 'bow trippers'. *David Clarke*

*Below:* The distinctive steeple in the left distance of this view is that of the North Church of Scotland, known locally as the 'pepperpot'. Since 1961 this building has been the home of the Aberdeen Arts Centre. Also in the background, to the right of tram No 28, is Marischal College, which is the second-largest granite building in the world. I sat my Animal Biology first year degree exam in Mitchell Hall one of the buildings that are still retained by the University of Aberdeen. No 28 is heading for the Bridge of Don, also on 11 July 1956. *David Clarke*

*Right:* **Glasgow Corporation had been approached to build the streamliners for Aberdeen, but it was not permitted to build trams for other operators. Then, when the tram system in Aberdeen was nearing its end, Aberdeen Corporation offered the streamliners to Glasgow, but unfortunately the city turned down this opportunity, sealing the fate of the cars. No 30 is seen at the south end of King Street on 11 July 1956.** *David Clarke*

*Below:* **Hazlehead Park was purchased by Aberdeen City in 1920 for the then princely sum of £40,000. Between March and October 1924, and with the cost subsidised by 50%, the three-quarters-of-a-mile private track to Hazlehead was built, opening on 16 July 1924. This view** of No 32 is at the Hazlehead terminus on 12 April 1955; at that time of the year the route terminated at Castle Street, as I suspect the Beach terminus in April would still be mighty cold. *David Clarke*

*Right:* **Passing under the Deeside railway bridge in Holburn Street on 11 July 1956, heading for Bridge of Don, is No 35. The Deeside railway line had been part of the Great North of Scotland Railway, and ran between Aberdeen and Ballater. It opened from Aberdeen to Banchory on 7 September 1853, was extended to Aboyne on 2 December 1859, and to Ballater on 17 October 1866. It was mostly single track with passing loops and was nicknamed 'The Subbies'. It became part of the LNER in 1923, then British Railways took over operations in 1948, but unfortunately, like so many railways, the Beeching Report sealed its fate and the last passenger service ran on 28 February 1966, with freight services finishing later that year. The film at the Odeon is** *The Maverick Queen,* **which starred Barbara Stanwyck and was released in the UK in mid-1956.** *David Clarke*

*Below:* **This is No 36 exiting the Castle Street sidings onto Union Street at rush hour on 10 July 1956. Nos 19 to 38 cost in excess of £11,000 each and were, in my opinion, beautiful trams. After withdrawal on 3 May 1958 all the Corporation trams were driven to Queens Links on the 12th and 13th and burned, cut up, squashed and taken to the scrapyard. The streamliners were only nine years old, and they were scrapped for £90. No 36 was the subject of an abortive preservation plan.** *David Clarke*

*Right:* **The last of the 20 streamliners to enter service was No 38 on 30 July 1949. Almost seven years later to the day, the tram is seen at the Sea Beach terminus. The sun is out, the beach car park is busy, the show is on at Hazlehead, and an elegant tram awaits customers. Today the tracks are still in place, partially tarred over, and the area is used as a car park.** *David Clarke*

*Below:* **Between March and June 1947 Aberdeen took delivery of nine Weymann-bodied AEC Regent IIIs, Nos 23 to 31 (BRS 523 to 531). Nos 23 to 26 were 'RT' type, while the remainder were 'Provincial' style, all costing £3,304 each. Exiting King Street depot in the early months of 1965 is No 30 (BRS 530). All of this batch of buses were rebuilt and reseated by the Corporation between 1960 and 1962. Nos 23 to 26 were withdrawn during 1966, while Nos 27 to 31 lasted until September 1967.**

*Right:* In March 1951 ten Daimler CVG6s with Northern Coachbuilders bodywork were delivered, numbered 160 to 169 (DRS 360 to 369). During 1960 they received new Alexander 66-seat bodies, and seen standing in King Street, near the entrance to the depot, is No 162 (DRS 362). In the background is one of the Metro-Cammell-bodied Daimler CVG6s, which were new in 1956. This view was taken in the summer of 1972, by which time only Nos 161 and 162 of the batch were still in service. No 162 was withdrawn in 1973 and purchased by Alexander (Greyhound) of Arbroath in July, probably for spares.

*Below:* During 1954, for tram replacement, the Corporation took delivery of 20 Daimler CVG6s, Nos 170 to 189 (GRG 170 to 189). Nos 170 to 174 were bodied by Metro-Cammell and the remainder by Crossley. Representing the Crossley batch at the Castlegate bus stance in September 1971 is No 182 (GRG 182). This bus was withdrawn in early 1972 and purchased by the Highland Gliding Club in Elgin in June. Queen Anne blended whisky was first produced in 1884 by Hill Thomson & Co Ltd. A 1980s bottle of Queen Anne can be yours for £24.95, and is, in my opinion, one of the finest blended whiskies.

*Right:* **During 1955 Aberdeen Corporation took delivery of its last Crossley-bodied Daimler CVG6s, Nos 190 to 204 and 210 to 214. Representing this batch is No 201 (HRG 201), which is working route 15 to Faulds Gate; it is seen in Guild Street when brand new. The Criterion pub is still there and is owned by the former Aberdeen and St Mirren football player Frank MacDougall. Brooke Bond tea was founded by Arthur Brooke in 1845 (there never was a 'Mr Bond'), and the company's most famous brand, PG Tips, was launched in 1930.** *transporttreasury. co.uk*

*Below:* **The five Crossley-bodied AEC Regent Vs that arrived during 1955 are my all-time favourite buses. Numbered 205 to 209 (HRG 205 to 209), they cost £4,205 when new and had Gardner 6LW engines. This is Guild Street in 1955, and the railway station is on the right of this view of No 205. Note the tram track to the left of the bus, a remnant of the Torry tram** route that closed on 28 February 1931. Nos 205 to 209 were all withdrawn in early 1971 and by August of that year Alexander (Greyhound) of Arbroath had purchased all five. They were all withdrawn by December 1974 and two, Nos 207 and 209, were later noted on a farm in the Dundee area. *transporttreasury.co.uk*

*Main picture:* **The date is 11 December 1974 and crossing the railway bridge on Guild Street is No 219 (JRG 219). This was one of a batch of 15 Metro-Cammell-bodied Daimler CVG6s, Nos 215 to 229 (JRG 215 to 229), that were delivered during 1956. Only Nos 218 to 221 and 229 passed to Grampian Regional Transport on 16 May 1975, and were subsequently noted at the yard of Whiting of Pontefract in October of that year.**

*Opposite top:* **Working route 18 to Summerhill in the summer of 1972 is another of the Metro-Cammell-bodied Daimler CVG6s that arrived during 1956, No 221 (JRG 221). The bus is crossing Union Bridge, which was built by Thomas Fletcher between 1801 and 1805. It is the largest single-span granite bridge in the world, at 40 metres. It was widened in 1908, and steel side spans, which carry today's pavements, were introduced. The bridge crosses the Denburn Valley and Union Terrace Gardens. The car beyond the double yellow line is a Ford Zodiac Mark III, which when tested in 1962 had a top speed of just over 100mph, did 0 to 60 in 13.4 seconds, and at that time cost £1,060 including taxes.**

*Below:* **Between May and June 1957 Aberdeen took delivery of 20 Metro-Cammell-bodied Daimler CVG6s at a cost of £4,882 each. They were numbered 230 to 249 (KRG 230 to 249), and descending Union Street in December 1973 is No 241 (KRG 241). The advert on the bus is for *The Scotsman*, a paper that was launched in Edinburgh as a weekly in 1817 and became a daily newspaper in 1850. To the left, under Trinity Hall, are McMillan's toy store and Timpsons Shoes, now a distant memory.**

*Right:* In October 1957 the Corporation took delivery of five Park Royal-bodied AEC Regent Vs, Nos 250 to 254 (KRS 250 to 254). They cost £4,800 each and were the only Park Royal-bodied buses ever purchased by Aberdeen Corporation. Representing this batch is No 254, working route 5 to Woodend in the summer of 1972. Christian Salvesen & Co was formed in 1872 in Leith, and initially operated as a shipping and forwarding agent, ship-broker and timber merchant. In the early 1900s the company developed significant interests in whaling, but discontinued that in 1963 and reinvented itself as a transport and logistics company; in 2007 it was merged with Norbert Dentressangle.

*Below:* On 3 May 1958 route 1 was operated by trams as usual until around 4.00pm. From then on the trams were gradually replaced by brand-new Metro-Cammell-bodied AEC Regent Vs, Nos 255 to 269 (KRS 255 to 269). These also served route 1, but the destinations were now Garthdee and Balgownie; the route followed the tram route, but now had extensions beyond Bridge of Dee and Bridge of Don. This is No 259 (KRS 259) in the summer of 1972, working the former tram route 4 to Hazlehead. All these buses were withdrawn in late 1975, and had reached the scrapyards of Pontefract and Barnsley by January 1976. Travelling in the opposite direction on route 25 is No 326 (CRG 326C), an Alexander-bodied Daimler CVG6 new in March 1965. Just behind No 259 is one of the Alexander-bodied Leyland PSUC1/13s, new in 1966.

*Right:* **Arriving in June 1959 were Nos 271 to 275 (MRS 271 to 275); they were AEC Regent Vs and were the first Alexander-bodied buses for the Corporation. Delivered with AEC engines, they were fitted with Gardner 6LW units in 1963. Seen leaving Castle Street in the summer of 1975 is No 275 (MRS 275). All five were withdrawn in 1976 and all five passed to Alexander (Greyhound). The bus behind, heading for Scatterburn, is No 29 (NRG 29H), an Alexander-bodied AEC Swift new in late 1969. The N-registered car is, I think, a Datsun Sunny.**

*Below:* **From 1960 until 1965 Aberdeen purchased 57 Daimler CVG6s, 45 of which were bodied by Alexander and 12 by Metro-Cammell. Representing the Alexander-bodied buses is No 316 (URG 316), one of a batch of 11 delivered between April and May 1963. The bus has just passed the railway and bus station in Guild Street in the summer of 1972.**

**No 316 remained in service until withdrawal in 1980, and was noted at the scrapyard of Whiting of Pontefract in September 1980. The taxi on the left is an H-registered Morris Oxford VI; a diesel-engined version was introduced in 1961, and was popular as a taxi. The Oxford VI remained in production until 1971, with just over 208,000 produced. The van behind the bus is the very recognisable pug-nosed Bedford CA, which was produced between 1952 and 1969.**

*Right:* The first conversion to one-person operation in Aberdeen was started in 1966, when six Alexander-bodied one-person-equipped Leyland PSUC1/13s were introduced on route 14 Footdee to Castle Street. The six, which had cost £5,138 each, were numbered 1 to 6 (ERG 1D to 6D), and seen working the now extended route 14 in the winter of 1971 is No 1. All six had been withdrawn and sold for scrap by February 1980.

*Above:* **During May 1964 eight Alexander-bodied Daimler CVG6s were delivered, Nos 317 to 324 (VRS 317 to 324). From this batch Nos 318 to 324 were rebuilt to forward entrance and fitted for one-person operation; the first completed was No 323 in 1968, and the last No 318 in 1972. This is No 317, the only one of the batch not converted to front entrance; it is seen leaving Castle Street for Mastrick in the summer of 1975. This bus was among the last of the Daimler CVG6s to be withdrawn in July 1982.**

*Left:* **The last half-cab buses purchased by Aberdeen arrived in March 1965, numbered 325 to 332 (CRG 325C to 332C). They cost £5,710 new, and seen working route 22 to Northfield in December 1973 is No 332.**

In July 1966 Aberdeen Corporation took delivery of its first rear-engined buses. They were Nos 100 to 111 (ERG 100D to 111D), had Alexander A-type bodywork, and cost £6,822 each. A national agreement between the trade unions and municipal operators in May 1969 allowed the introduction of one-person operation, and Nos 100 to 111 were equipped for this during 1970. This is No 102 (ERG 102D) in Skye Road in August 1978. The parked car is a Vauxhall Viva HC, which when launched would set you back £783, took 20.6 seconds to reach 60mph, and was flat out at 78mph.

*Above:* Working route 25 in Union Street in the summer of 1972 is No 109 (ERG 109D). The car passing the Gloucester Hotel is a Vauxhall Victor FD Series, just over 198,000 of which were produced between 1967 and 1972. When new it cost £819, did 0 to 60mph in 14 seconds, and was flat out at 95mph. Buses Nos 100 to 107 were withdrawn in 1978, and the remainder had been withdrawn by October of the following year.

*Below:* Nos 7 to 12 (GRS 7E to 12E) were Alexander Y-type-bodied Leyland PSUC1/13s that arrived during June 1967. This view of No 10 (GRS 10E) working route 6 was taken in the summer of 1972. All six were withdrawn in 1979, and four, Nos 7/8/10 and 12, were sold to Peace of Kirkwall in June of that year, while at the same time No 11 passed to Leask of Lerwick. No 10 is now in preservation.

*Right:* In 1967 Aberdeen Corporation switched its single-deck purchases to AEC, and ten Alexander W-type-bodied Swifts arrived during June of that year. They were numbered 15 to 24 (JRS 15F to 24F), and working service 14 in the summer of 1971 is No 15 (JRS 15F). I particularly like the frontal styling of the Alexander W-type body. All were withdrawn by 1981, with a number passing to Aberdeen District Council. The Daytona Yellow car in the background is a Ford Capri Mark I, first introduced to the public at the Brussels Motor Show in January 1969. The Capri was an inexpensive and practical four-seater with the lines of a sports fastback. A bewildering array of options and accessories could be specified by the owner, in effect making each Capri almost tailor-made to an individual's taste, starting with 32 basic derivatives and with a choice of six engines, (1300, 1600, 1300GT, 1600GT, 2000GT and 3000GT). A 1600GT in good order today can cost around £8,000, when the asking price back in 1969 was £1,066 12s 11d.

*Top:* During September and October 1970 another 15 dual-doorway AEC Swifts with Alexander W-type bodies arrived, Nos 25 to 39 (NRG 25H to 39H). Working the Kincorth Circular in the summer of 1971 is No 26 (NRG 26H). All this batch were withdrawn by 1982, and No 26 was acquired by Aberdeen District Council in June 1981.

*Right:* **In April 1971 the Bridges route was converted to one-person operation using 33-foot Daimler CRG6LXs with Alexander L-type dual-doorway bodies, which cost £9,804 each. They were numbered 122 to 141 (PRG 122J to 141J), and working route 1 to Balgownie in Union Street in the summer of 1971 is No 125 (PRG 125J). The white car following the bus is a Wolseley 6/110, of which just over 24,000 were produced between 1961 and 1968. This car is a Mark II, which was available from May 1964, and at that time cost £1,179. It was flat out at 102mph, did 0 to 60 in 13.3 seconds, was quite thirsty at 19 miles per gallon, and was a popular and well-liked car with many police forces.**

*Above:* Heading for Garthdee in the summer of 1971 is No 139 (PRG 139J), another of the same batch, new in March 1971. All these buses had been withdrawn by 1982, but a number saw further service with other operators.

*Opposite top:* During August 1964 Leeds Corporation took delivery of four dual-doorway AEC Reliances bodied by Roe and numbered 44 to 47 (44 to 47 KUA). During 1971 they were acquired by Aberdeen Corporation for the princely sum of £800 each. By the time this photograph was taken in early 1974 one-person operation had been introduced on around 60% of the Corporation's operations. By May 1975, out of a fleet of 247 buses, 138 were one-person operated. Nos 44 to 47 were withdrawn from service in 1976, and by November of that year were with Dunsmore of Larkhall. Wilson of Carnwath purchased three, Nos 44, 45 and 47, in December 1976, and they remained with that independent operator until being noted derelict or withdrawn in September 1982. Seen here is No 46 (46 KUA).

*Right:* Descending Guild Street in March 1974 is No 171 (NRG 171M), one of a batch of 24 Alexander-bodied Leyland AN68/1Rs delivered to the Corporation between November 1973 and January 1974. Nos 154 to 177 cost £12,159 each and were the last new double-deck buses purchased by the Corporation before the fleet passed to Grampian Regional Transport on 16 May 1975.

# Dundee Corporation

The first tram line was built by Dundee Corporation in 1877 and was leased to Dundee & District Tramways. Horse traction began on 30 August 1877, and after trials with a steam engine and carriage the first engine and car started on 20 June 1885. In 1897 Dundee Corporation began negotiations to purchase the Dundee & District tramway system, and the undertaking was acquired on 1 June 1899. On taking control, the Corporation began to electrify the system, which was completed with the withdrawal of the last steam wagon on 14 May 1902.

Powers to operate buses and trolleybu were obtained in 1907, and trolleyl operation began on 5 September 1912, only lasted until the 13 May 1914. Corporation's first buses were purcha in 1921 and began operations betw Dundee and Broughty Ferry, but a legal protestations by the Broughty Fe & District Tramways these ceased or July 1922, and the buses began operat of a circular route from the city centre Stobswell on 20 September. In Decem

uthority was given to the Tramways Department to construct its own tramcars. The next buses, Leyland Lions, were placed n service in January 1927. The joint tram oute to Broughty Ferry, which had been n operation since 27 December 1905, eased when the Corporation purchased he Broughty Ferry company on 15 May 1931, and bus operations started the next lay. Bus services became established from 1930 to 1939, and post-war developments ncluded new services to Blackness via ochee Road, Blackshade, Mains of intry, St Marys and Camperdown via ochee Road.

In September 1954 the Corporation lecided to withdraw the Blackness to Downfield tram route as an experiment. A fleet of Daimler CVG6s took over the ervice on 27 November 1955, and within ix months the decision had been made to vithdraw the remaining tram services. In order to avoid waiting for new buses, 30

Craven-bodied former London Transport AEC Regent IIIs were purchased from Bird's of Stratford-upon-Avon. The last trams ran on 20 October 1956 and the withdrawn cars were sold for scrap in part exchange for the Regent IIIs.

From 1957 through to 1960 Daimler CVG6s were purchased and, with a view to one-person operation, ten AEC Reliances were ordered in 1961. However, due to problems with one-person operation, these buses were not bodied until 1964 and did not enter service until 1966. Meanwhile, following trials with Daimler Fleetline 4559 VC in April 1963, large-capacity double-deckers were delivered to the Corporation fleet in January 1965. One-person operation, after some difficulties in August 1968, began with single-deck buses on 13 April 1969 and, after trails in 1972, double-deck one-person operation began on routes 1, 1a and 2 in January 1973.

**Trams Nos Tram Nos 1 to 10 were supplied for the opening of the system in 1900. They were originally open-top with five windows and short canopies, but received top covers between 1907 and 1910, and were rebuilt as all-enclosed between 1930 and 1931. This is tram No 2 at the junction of Kingsway and Strathmartine Road at 10.33am on 10 April 1955.** *David Clarke*

*Above:* **During 1921 Dundee Corporation took delivery of eight trams built by Hurst Nelson. They were originally numbered 83 to 90, were renumbered 47 to 54 in 1928, and finally to Nos 34 to 40 and 51 in 1936. They were all rebuilt and retrucked during 1932 and 1933. This is tram No 36 at the west end of the High Street on 9 July 1956. The advertisement on the front is for Abdine, 'The Gold Medal Health Drink'.** *David Clarke*

*Left:* **Only every third tram went to Ninewells, which gave a 12-minute frequency to that terminus. This is tram No 39 on Perth Road near Ninewells on 9 July 1956. When rebuilt, it was fitted with EMB flexible axle trucks and DK20A 40hp motors. The car on the right is a Standard Eight. To keep prices down, the car at launch was very basic with sliding windows, a single windscreen wiper and no external boot lid – access to the boot was by folding down the rear seat, which had the backrest divided in two. The 1954 Deluxe model had wind-up windows, and the Gold Star model of 1957 an opening boot lid. From mid-1955 all the Eights had wind-up windows. At launch the Standard Eight cost £481 including taxes and had a top speed of 61mph.** *David Clarke*

During 1916 four Hurst Nelson trams were delivered, and all were rebuilt in 1932 and received EMB flexible axle trucks and DK105/1C 50hp motors. The four were renumbered 47 to 50 in 1936. On the Perth Road at West Park is No 47, also on 9 July 1956. Two out of three trams turned at West Park. Did you know that the 'Golly' for Golden Shred was first introduced by Robertson's in 1910 on items such as price lists and labels, and was finally retired in 2002. During 2012 Paddington Bear was signed to appear on Robertson's Golden Shred marmalade. *David Clarke*

*Right:* **During 1902 eight Milnes-built trams, Nos 41 to 48, entered service; they were top-covered by 1907, and renumbered 11 to 18 in 1927. Nos 11 and 12 were rebuilt in 1928 and received Peckham P35 trucks and DK105/1C 50hp motors; both later received EMB flexible axle trucks. This is tram No 12 in High Street on 9 April 1955. The advertisement on the front of the tram is for Bovril, which 'Cheers and Invigorates'. Due to the transportation and storage problems with foreign-produced beef, in 1870 John Lawson Johnston created a product called 'Johnston's Fluid Beef', which later became known as Bovril.** *David Clarke*

*Below:* **During 1920 six Hurst Nelson-built trams were delivered, Nos 67, 68 and 79 to 82. They were renumbered 41 to 46 in 1928 and rebuilt during 1932 and 1933. This is tram No 46 at Blackness terminus, also on 9 April 1955. De Reszke cigarettes were named after Jean de Reszke (1850-1925), a famous Polish** opera-singer, and were advertised as 'the Aristocrat of Cigarettes'. They were produced by J. Millhoff & Co of Piccadilly, a Russian cigarette-maker living in London. He created a special blend of tobacco that, it was believed, would not damage the famous singer's voice. In gratitude, Millhoff was allowed to sell the blend as 'De Reszke' cigarettes. *David Clarke*

*Above:* This is tram No 39, new in 1921 and rebuilt during 1932-33, at the junction of Dens Road and Main Street on 11 April 1955. Dens Road is the location of Dens Park, the home of Dundee Football Club since 1899. *David Clarke*

*Below:* Trams Nos 1 to 10 were rebuilt more than once, and were withdrawn in 1955 after a remarkable 55 years in service. This is No 10 at the junction of Main Street and Strathmartine Road on the same day. The advertisement on the front of the tram is for Millar's 'Confectionery of Quality'. John Millar & Sons of Edinburgh had been making confectionery, such as Millar's Pan Drops, since 1884, and have recently been bought out of administration by Nisha Enterprises. *David Clarke*

*Right:* **Working the Downfield route is tram No 15, seen on Strathmartine Road at its junction with Clepington Road on 11 April 1955. The terminus at Downfield was the highest, at 328 feet above sea level.** *David Clarke*

*Below:* **The pride of the Dundee Corporation tram fleet were Nos 19 to 28, the 'Lochee Cars', supplied by Brush in 1930. They were intended for use on the Ninewells to Maryfield route, but Dundee's narrow track spacing precluded them passing each other with safety, and they were transferred to the Reform Street to Lochee route, where they remained for their entire operating life, except for occasional special hires by enthusiasts. This is tram No 23 at Lochee terminus on 9 July 1956. Note the** advertisement for Red & White cigarettes, 'for the man who inhales'. Red & White cigarettes are produced by Philip Morris International and are quite popular in European markets. *David Clarke*

*Right:* **This is Lochee High Street on 9 July 1956, and the approaching tram is Brush-built No 26. The two vans are, on the left, a Ford Thames 300E, and to the right of the tram a Morris Minor; the latter was first built in 1953 and continued in production until 1971, being purchased in significant numbers by the Post Office.** *David Clarke*

*Below:* **At Lochee railway station, also on 9 July 1956, is Brush-built tram No 24. The bridge in the background carries the Dundee to Newtyle railway line, which was the first in the north of Scotland, with regular passenger services commencing on 16 December 1831. The completion of the Lochee deviation, which removed the Law incline from the route, was completed in 1861. Passenger** services on the Newtyle branch ceased on 10 January 1955. Aitken's beer was brewed in Falkirk; the company was founded in 1740 and survived until 1960, when the business became part of Caledonian United Breweries, later Tennant Caledonian. The Falkirk brewery at Newmarket Street lasted until 1968 and the buildings were demolished in 1970. *David Clarke*

*Above:* **This is Brush-built tram No 23 in Logie Street on 9 July 1956. Apart from the short length of track in Lochee High Street, the climb to Lochee terminus, which was 279 feet above sea level, was a climb all the way, with a maximum gradient of 1 in 16 at Mitchell Street.** *David Clarke*

*Below:* **There is not much room for Brush-built Nos 21 and 25 to pass on Lochee Road, as seen on the same day. The van parked at the roadside is a Fordson E494C 5cwt, which was powered by an 8hp 933cc side-valve engine. By the end of production in July 1954 more than 66,000 of this model had been built.** *David Clarke*

*Above:* **Dundee Corporation built a new depot and works in Lochee Road, which opened in July 1900. With the abandonment of trams in 1956 the depot was closed for traffic and used as a store from October of that year. Here we see Brush-built No 24 at Lochee depot on 9 July 1956.** *David Clarke*

*Below:* **This is Brush-built tram No 20 at the junction of Ward Road and North Tay Street on the same day.** *David Clarke*

*Above:* **Brush-bodied tram No 27 was photographed in North Lindsay Street on 9 July 1956. All the Brush-bodied trams had EMB trucks and DK105/1C 50hp motors. At peaks hours the Lochee route ran a 3-minute frequency, with a 4-minute service off-peak, and at peak times 11 trams were in use. The downhill trip was scheduled to be completed in 12½ minutes, while the uphill return trip took 19 minutes.** *David Clarke*

for Lee's Macaroon Bars. John Justice Lee, a grocer's son from Coatbridge, first produced this bar in 1931, and the company was sold to Northumbrian Fine Foods in 1991. *David Clarke*

*Right:* **Working towards the city centre from Maryfield at Albert Street on the same day is tram No 39. In the background is the Ogilvie and Stobswell Parish Church, which was built between 1874 and 1876. The advert on the front of No 39 is**

*Right:* **At the junction of Forfar Road and Madeira Street is tram No 38. If you look carefully in the background you can see buses standing at Maryfield depot, and Morgan Academy is only a few yards away. The tram is adverting Luxor Sauce, 'Good with all meals'.** *David Clarke*

*Below:* **Passing Maryfield depot on 9 July 1956 is tram No 48. Maryfield depot was first used in June 1901, and when the trams ceased operating in October 1956 it continued to be used as a bus depot. It had limited engineering facilities, and closed operationally for buses, I think, in 1972. However, the depot remained in Dundee Corporation, later Tayside Regional Council, ownership, and was brought back into use in the late 1970s for engineering, primarily bodywork and some painting, when the** facilities at East Dock Street proved to be less than adequate for modern vehicles. After final use for buses in the 1980s, Maryfield depot was used by other local authority services until vacated a few years ago. It remains vacant, and there are plans to use it as the basis of a Transport Museum. *David Clarke*

*Above:* **This is Maryfield terminus on 9 July 1956 – nearest the camera is No 34, with No 42 in the distance. During the mid-1920s a proposal was put forward to extend the tramway from Maryfield terminus to Kingsway, then west for a quarter of a** mile to the golf course at Caird Park, which unfortunately did not take place. *David Clarke*

*Below:* **At the junction of Arbroath Road and Princes Street on the same July day in 1956 is tram No 40.** *David Clarke*

**Above:** This is Nethergate at the junction of South Tay Street on 9 July 1956, and heading for West Park is tram No 38. *David Clarke*

**Below:** This is tram No 35 on Perth Road at West Wynd on the same date. The car parked to the left is another Standard Eight, described on page 48. The first electric tram ran from the High Street to Ninewells via Nethergate and Perth Road on 12 July 1900. *David Clarke*

*Left:* **This is tram No 34 on Perth Road at the junction of Fords Lane on 9 July 1956. The peak of the Dundee tram system was in 1932, but by 1951 many of the trams had not been updated, and at least a third of the fleet was more than 50 years old. A study by the Belfast transport consultant Colonel R. McCreary said that the cost of running trams compared with bus services was nearly 5½ pence per mile greater, and he concluded that the tramway system should be abandoned in 1952.** *David Clarke*

*Right:* **Tram No 47 stands at the West Park Road short working terminus on the same day. Behind it is West Park Hall student residences, halls that were traditionally popular with medicine students due to their proximity to Ninewells Hospital. The residences consist of a relatively new complex known as West Park Villas, which are essentially student flats. The old hall, separate from the Villas, was largely demolished in 2005, leaving behind only the listed parts of the building.** *David Clarke*

*Below:* **Arriving in Dundee from Perth in the early 1950s the enthusiast would find, on most occasions, the first Dundee tram standing at the single-track terminus at Ninewells. The tracks ended precisely at the city boundary, and here we see tram No 46 at the terminus on 9 July 1956.** *David Clarke*

*Left:* **Trams of all varieties were used to supplement the Brush-built trams Nos 19 to 28 on the Lochee route. Standing at the Lochee terminus on 11 July 1956 are, nearest the camera, No 22, then Nos 41 and 23. Just visible behind the trees on the left is Lochee West Church, which had James McLaren as architect. Building began in October 1869, and the church was officially opened on 24 September 1871.** *David Clarke*

*Above:* **This is No 40 in Cowgate on 11 July 1956. To the right of the view is the Gaumont, which began as The Kings Theatre & Hippodrome and opened on 15 March 1909. Designed by architect Frank Thomson in a mix of Baroque and Rococo styles, the auditorium seated 2,227 in stalls, dress circle and balcony, with boxes on each side of the stage. It was taken over by Provincial Cinematograph Theatres (PCT), opening as a cinema on 24 September 1928. A Wurlitzer two-manual, six-rank organ was installed, with the console on a lift. The seating capacity was reduced to 1,458 by closing the balcony seating area. In February 1929 PCT was taken over by Gaumont British Theatres Ltd and the cinema was renamed the Gaumont from 8 May 1950. In 1961 the interior was entirely rebuilt: a suspended ceiling was inserted at balcony level and the side walls and proscenium were covered over. Most of the original decoration was retained, but was now totally hidden from view. It was** renamed the Odeon, but closed on 24 October 1981, and the building was converted into a bingo club from May 1983. I think it is now a bar/night club. *David Clarke*

*Below:* **This is No 47 at the junction of Murraygate and Commercial Street, also on 11 July 1956. Smith Brothers (Dundee Ltd) was a long-established draper and clothier, and on the third floor were the luncheon and tea rooms. I think the store closed in the 1970s and became John Menzies.** *David Clarke*

*Right:* **Very few trams other than the Brush-built Nos 19 to 28 received the simplified final livery style. This is tram No 50 sporting the new livery in Reform Street on the same day in 1956. In the distance is the Caird Hall, named after the jute producer James Key Caird and built between 1914 and 1923. The Caird Hall has hosted the Royal Scottish National Orchestra and is used for graduation ceremonies. I have to admit that I was at Caird Hall on the night of 27 January 1973, at a cost of £3 for the front area, to see Led Zeppelin!** *David Clarke*

*Below:* **This is tram No 37 at Nethergate on 11 July 1956. Behind the tram are the Royal Hotel and the Atholl Hotel, and to the right, just out of view, is Green's Playhouse then St Paul's Church. Green's Playhouse was a large cinema** opened in 1936 and was second only in size in the UK to Green's Playhouse in Glasgow. Note the centre poles, which were painted shining silver and dated from the electrification of the trams in Dundee in 1900. *David Clarke*

*Above:* **Between late 1951 and early 1952 Dundee Corporation took delivery of 10 Croft-bodied Daimler CVD6s, which when new were fitted with 8.4-litre Daimler engines. They were numbered 125 to 134 (AYJ 377 to 379 and BTS 468 to 474), and seen at Dock Street in the summer of 1971 is No 126 (AYJ 378). This bus was withdrawn from public service during the following year, but became driver trainer T2, and as such passed to Tayside Regional Council on 16 May 1975.**

*Below:* **During 1949 Dundee took delivery of 10 Barnard-bodied Daimler CVD6s, which also had the 8.4-litre Daimler engine; they were Nos 121 to 124 (ATS 901 to 904) and 115 to 120 (ATS 905 to 910). The whole batch received new Alexander bodies during 1959 and 1960. Seen at Dock Street in the summer of 1971 is No 118 (ATS 908), which received its new body in 1960 and remained in the fleet until sold for scrap to Dunsmore of Larkhall in 1972.**

*Above:* **Also photographed at Dock Street in the summer of 1971 is No 76 (CTS 635), a Weymann-bodied Daimler CVD6 that was part of a batch of 10 received in 1953. It was withdrawn from service in 1972 and sold for scrap the following year. However, four of this batch, Nos 70, 74, 78 and 79, survived to 1975, becoming the last exposed-radiator Daimlers still working in a Scottish fleet.**

*Below:* **Seven Alexander-bodied AEC Regent IIIs with AEC A218 engines were delivered between August and September 1953. They were numbered 135 to 141 (CYJ 250 to 256), and this is No 136 (CYJ 251), which remained in the fleet until 1974. No 137 (CYJ 252) was transferred as a withdrawn bus to Tayside Regional Council in May 1975 and still survives.**

*Above:* **Working a schools service in the autumn of 1969 is No 138 (CYJ 253), an Alexander-bodied AEC Regent III new in September 1953. This bus was withdrawn in 1974 and sold to Dunsmore of Larkhall, being noted at their yard in May 1975. The van on the left is delivering for Fisher & Donaldson, one of Scotland's best-known craft bakers which has premises in Cupar, St Andrews and Dundee.** *Phil Sposito*

**on the Blackness to Downfield route. They were the mainstay of this service until 1966, when new Daimler CRG6LXs Nos 35 to 54 arrived. At that point Nos 180 to 204 became regular performers on a number of Dundee routes. The Corporation purchased 88 Daimler CVG6s between 1955 and 1960, and all but a handful remained in service long after Tayside Regional Council took control in May 1975.**

*Right:* **No 180 (ETS 960), seen here leaving Dock Street in the summer of 1971, was delivered new to Dundee Corporation in November 1955 and was part of a batch of 25 Metro-Cammell-bodied Daimler CVG6s, numbered 180 to 204 (ETS 960 to 984). These buses entered service on 27 November 1955 when they took over operations from the tram cars**

*Above:* **Working service 1 and passing Seagate in the autumn of 1968 is No 188 (ETS 968), a Metro-Cammell-bodied Daimler CVG6 new to Dundee in 1955 and passed to the Tayside Regional Council fleet on 16 May 1975. It was renumbered 72 in 1977 and was withdrawn and sold to Hartwood of Barnsley shortly afterwards. The car, partly visible, travelling behind is a Wolseley 16/60, which was first produced in Cowley in 1961, and just over 63,000 were produced until 1971. The launch price was £993, but you had to put up with no synchromesh in first gear. Viewed from the outside, the 16/60 was differentiated from the 15/60 by the overriders on the bumpers, which protruded more than on the earlier car, and the plastic mouldings on the rear lights were also modified together with the rear fins, which were now slightly reduced in their sharpness.** *Phil Sposito*

*Right:* **A few months before the last trams ran in Dundee on 20 October 1956, six Park**

**Royal-bodied Daimler CVG6s were delivered to the Corporation. They were numbered 205 to 210 (FTS 209 to 214), and representing this batch in the summer of 1971 is No 205 (FTS 209). Did you know that C&A was founded by brothers Clemens and August Brenninkmeijer as a Dutch textile company in 1841? The retail stores in the UK were first established in 1922, and the last closed its doors in 2001.**

The last traditional half-cab buses delivered new to Dundee, Alexander-bodied Daimler CVG6s with pre-selective gearboxes, arrived in June 1960, and were originally numbered 96 to 102 (KTS 96 to 102). In 1964 Nos 96 to 99 were renumbered 104, 103, 106 and 105 respectively, and working a service to Ninewells in 1971 is No 105 (KTS 99). Boots, the famous chain of chemist shops, was founded in Nottingham in 1849 by John Boot.

*Above:* A batch of 10 AEC Reliance 2U2RAs, Nos 25 to 34 (CTS 125D to 134D), was ordered in 1961 with a view to one-person operation, but they were not bodied by Alexander until 1964, and did not enter service until August 1966, as crew-operated buses. One-person operation eventually began on 11 August 1966, but due to strike action by crews it ceased on the 14th. Agreement was not reached until the summer of 1968, and it was not until 13 April 1969 that Dundee Corporation started one-person operation. This is No 29 (CTS 129D), seen just a few days after the transfer of Corporation buses to Tayside Regional Council in May 1975. I think the roofbox destination display does not do the Alexander Y-type bodywork any favours.

*Right:* The next single-deck buses to arrive were Nos 55 to 64, AEC Swifts with dual-doorway Alexander W-type bodywork. On delivery they carried registration numbers FTS 855F to 864F, but these

were changed to GYJ 455G to 464G before entry into service. The Swifts were largely unloved in Dundee; the lower driving position was disliked by drivers, and mechanically they were fragile in comparison to earlier and later single-deckers. No 56 (GYJ 456G) is depicted here wearing the two-tone green livery and working the Cross City service 13 in May 1975. By 1976 these buses were largely confined to lightly loaded works or school journeys and peak-hour reliefs.

This Daimler CRG6LX is No 288 (GYJ 488G), fitted with Alexander J-type bodywork and delivered to Dundee Corporation in August 1968. It was part of a batch of 15 with the fleet numbers 281 to 295, which were first registered FTS 881F to 895F. Because of the dispute over the introduction of one-person operation, only Nos 281 to 285 entered service, while the remainder were placed in storage. Nos 286 to 295 were then reregistered GYJ 486G to 495G before entering service. Daimler CRG6LX No 87 (AYJ 87B) was run experimentally as a one-person bus in 1972, and double-deck one-person operation began with the conversion of routes 1, 1a and 2 in January 1973. This view of No 288 (GYJ 488G) was taken in May 1975.

*Above:* **During 1970 Dundee took delivery of 25 Daimler SRG6LXs with Alexander W-type dual-doorway bodies. They were Nos 211 to 235 (KTS 211H to 235H), and working route 7 in the summer of 1971 is No 215 (KTS 215H). Its two-tone green livery, which in my opinion is quite attractive, and is similar to the Leeds Corporation livery, was applied to one-person-operated buses. Nos 211 to 235 were allocated to the 7/8 Circular, 10/11 Barnhill and 13/14 Cross City services, and were very fast free-running buses. However, most of the batch required attention after only a few years in service, and a few were rebuilt locally or by** Alexanders, while four were rebodied by Marshalls when about 10 years old.

*Below:* **In 1974-75 Dundee purchased 15 Metro-Cammell Orion-bodied Leyland PD2/20s from Edinburgh Corporation. Edinburgh had purchased 300 of these buses between 1954 and 1957 and for more than a decade they were the mainstay of the city's fleet. As part of the conditions of the sale, the 15 buses were overhauled and repainted, and seen at Dock Street depot in early 1975 is former Edinburgh Corporation No 488 (LFS 488), which was renumbered 4 by Dundee Corporation.**

# Edinburgh Corporation

The Edinburgh Street Tramways Company began a horse tram line between Bernard Street and Haymarket on 6 November 1871, and the system was extended over a number of years. Edinburgh Corporation purchased the company in 1893. In 1888 the Edinburgh Northern Tramways Company opened its first route in Hanover Street using cable traction. This company was also purchased by the Corporation, in 1896, then both purchased concerns were leased to a new company called the Edinburgh & District Tramways, which converted all the horse routes to cable traction. By the end of the conversion Edinburgh had the fourth largest cable tram system in the world. The lease to Edinburgh & District ceased on 30 June 1919, and the Corporation took over tramway operations. With the extension of the city boundaries in 1920, Edinburgh gained control of Leith Corporation Tramways on 20 November of that year.

The first Edinburgh Corporation bus entered service on 3 August 1914, and in June 1922 the first double-deck open-topped bus entered service. In the latter year the Corporation decided to convert the cable tram system to overhead electric, which was completed in only 53 weeks. On 20 June 1923 the first through electric tram ran between Edinburgh and Leith, and three days later the last cable car ran between the Post Office and Portobello. The next day electric trams ran between the Post Office and Port Seton.

On 12 December 1904 Musselburgh & District began to run electric trams between Levenhall and Joppa. This company ceased operations on 1 March 1928, and

Heading east along Princes Street on route 16 between Granton and Fairmilehead on 3 July 1956 is tram No 210. This tram and Nos 59, 73, 217 and 224 were the only ones built by Shrubhill in 1947; this decline in production was largely due to pressure of work on buses and older trams. *David Clarke*

Levenhall became the end of the line for Corporation trams. The tramway system remained intact through the war and the buses opened up new routes to districts such as Cramond, Niddrie, Lochend and Blackhall. The first closed-top bus was obtained in 1933, and pre-war purchases were Daimler COG6s. During the war Guy Arabs were added to the fleet, together with Daimler CWG5s and CWA6s, and Bedford OBs.

The first tram withdrawal was route 24, which was converted to bus operations on 1 June 1952. On 25 September of that year the decision was made to abandon the tram system altogether and replace it with buses. For tram replacements, large numbers of Leyland Titans were purchased, together with 60 Guy Arabs from London Transport, given new bodies in 1952 and 1953. The tram system ran for the last time on 16 November 1956, and 70 Alexander-bodied Guy Arab IVs delivered during that year also hastened its demise.

Leyland Titans continued to be purchased through to 1966, and a large fleet of Leyland Tiger Cubs was purchased during 1959 and 1960 for routes with lighter traffic or low bridges. In 1966 the Corporation introduced rear-engine double-deckers, and the first one-person-operated double-deck bus began operations in October 1969.

*Left:* No 221 is working route 28 at the junction of Princes Street with Fredrick Street on 3 July 1956. This was one of eight trams that entered service in 1939. The van partially hidden by the traffic policeman on the left is a Morris J, which was produced between 1949 and 1961. The car heading east is a Hillman Minx four-door saloon, and passing No 221 is an Austin A40 Somerset, which was in production between 1952 and 1954. *David Clarke*

*Below:* The city was expanding in the 1920s and 1930s, but buses were an easier way to serve new housing estates like Craigmillar and Pilton. There were, however, some tramway extensions, and these included from Braids to Fairmilehead. This is tram No 248 at Braids terminus on 12 July 1956, a scene that has remained virtually unchanged apart from the removal of the tramline and wires. No 248 was one of seven cars that entered service in 1937. *David Clarke*

*Opposite top:* **This is tram No 41, photographed on the same day near Fairmilehead. It was one of 12 Shrubhill Standard cars that entered service in 1936.** *David Clarke*

*Left:* **By the end of 1937 Shrubhill had built 46 of the new Standard cars. Material was then ordered for a further 38 to replace all the remaining former cable cars. The new material differed in minor details only, but included the use of brown seating and panelling in the upper saloon and moquette seating in the lower saloon. This is tram No 216, which was new in 1939, at Fairmilehead on 12 July 1956; in the background is No 41.** *David Clarke*

*Above:* **Leeds Forge built 56 trams for Edinburgh Corporation during 1923, and they were originally four-window saloons, top-covered with extended canopies; all were later totally enclosed. Working route 20, in its rebuilt form, is No 97 at Joppa on 3 April 1953.** *David Clarke*

*Top:* **Nearest the camera in this picture taken on the same day on North Bridge is No 68, a Shrubhill-built tram that had totally enclosed balconies and entered service in 1932. The other tram in view is rebuilt Leeds Forge car No 302. North Bridge was constructed by Sir William Arrol & Co, is 525 feet long and 75 feet wide, and was officially opened on 15 September 1897.** *David Clarke*

*Centre:* **During 1934 Metro-Cammell delivered six all-steel cars with domed roofs and Maley & Taunton trucks. They were numbered 241, 242, 244 to 246 and 249, and seen at Granton on 17 April 1954 is No 242. The tram in the background, providing a contrast in build, is No 152, a Shrubhill tram that was also new in 1934.** *David Clarke*

*Bottom:* **This is tram No 57, which was new in 1928, at North High Street, Musselburgh, at the junction of Bridge Street on 19 July 1954. In the background is the Hayweights, which was once a well-known town symbol and landmark. Erected in the 1880s, it was originally used for weighing hay, but towards the end of its life was used as a weighbridge for sand and gravel. The clock was added in 1908, and stood for more than 60 years at this prominent intersection, near where the Brunton Hall now stands. The Hayweights was demolished in the late 1960s, and the clock languished in a builder's yard before being stored by the local authority at Macmerry; the mechanism is now in the clock tower at Eskmills.** *David Clarke*

*Above:* **Between 1929 and 1930 Shrubhill built Nos 367 to 371, with No 367 having the distinction of being the first new car with a fully enclosed top deck, entering service in August 1929. As new, the five had totally enclosed top-deck saloons, without bulkheads, and tubular electric heaters were fitted. At Musselburgh Tolbooth and Town Hall on 19 July 1954 is tram No 368. The Tolbooth dates from 1590 and the clock tower is dated 1496. The current building is said to have been constructed using stone from Our Lady of Loretto Chapel, which was demolished in the years following the Reformation, and comprises three floors with an extension to the north-east built between 1731 and 1733. A three-bay facade, designed by William Constable, was added between 1900 and 1901.** *David Clarke*

*Below:* **Musselburgh had its own electrified tram system from 1906, and until 1923 passengers had to change to the cable-hauled Edinburgh trams at Joppa. The Musselburgh system was subsequently incorporated into the Edinburgh system, with the tramway to Port Seton closing east of Levenhall in 1928. At Levenhall terminus, also on 19 July 1954, is tram No 68, which was built new, totally enclosed, at Shrubhill in 1932.** *David Clarke*

*Top:* **This is tram No 196 at Hermitage Place on 19 July 1954. To the right of this view is Leith Links, a public park that extends to around 46 acres. Its main claim to fame is records made in 1457 in relation to the banning of 'gauf' – this is the earliest known reference to the game of golf and, since it mentions banning the game, it would suggest that golf predates 1457.** *David Clarke*

*Centre:* **During 1935 Edinburgh Corporation took delivery of six semi-streamlined cars built by English Electric, Nos 19 to 24. All five initially had Peckham trucks, but Nos 21 to 24 later received Maley & Taunton trucks. Note that the English Electric trams had the route number box installed at the front behind the main panel with the route colour discs on the front offside. At the junction of Leith Walk and Pilrig Street is tram No 22. The church in the background is Pilrig St Paul's, designed by Peddie & Kinnear and constructed between 1861 and 1863.** *David Clarke*

*Bottom:* **At Firrhill on 20 July 1954 is, on the left, tram No 17, a Hurst Nelson-bodied car new in 1935, and, providing a contrast, No 80, a Shrubhill fully enclosed Standard new in 1933.** *David Clarke*

*Above:* **Hurst Nelson built eight trams for the Corporation in 1935, Nos 11 to 18, and working route 10 to Granton at Firrhill on the same day is No 11.** *David Clarke*

*Below:* **This is tram No 73, one of five built in 1947, at Craigmillar Park on 8 April 1955.** *David Clarke*

*Above:* **Tram No 45 is seen in Lady Road on the same day. Following it is one of the 60 wartime Guy Arab buses bought by the Corporation from London Transport in 1952. The chassis of these buses were dismantled and completely reconditioned in Shrubhill, and they were fitted with no-frills ultra-lightweight bodies by Duple/Nudd. Delivery of the completed buses commenced early in 1953, and they were initially used to replace tram services on routes 3 and 4.** *David Clarke*

*Below:* **Route 7 ran down Leith Walk into Junction Street, then turned west into Ferry Road and north into Stanley Road, where the terminus was situated between two short stretches of single line. The tracks, however, continued down Craighall Road to Newhaven Road, but had been unused since before the start of through electric working from Edinburgh. In October 1949 this section was again put into operation and the Stanley Road terminus became the foot of Craighall Road. No 21, a Metro-Cammell semi-streamlined tram new in 1935, is in Craighall Road on 8 April 1955.** *David Clarke*

*Above:* **The Shrubhill Standards were produced in large numbers in 1935, with a total of 26 entering service. No 165 was new in that year and is caught by the camera at the junction of Newhaven Road and Ferry Road on the same day as the previous photograph.** *David Clarke*

*Below:* **Routes 13 and 14 covered an identical route, but in opposite directions. The 13 route was from Churchill along Grange Road and down the Bridges and Leith Walk to Pilrig, turning left to reach Granton by way of Pilrig Street, Ferry Road and Granton Road. The routes then ran along Lower Granton Road to Newhaven, Bernard Street and Leith Walk. At the Post Office the route lay by the West End to Churchill. Route 14 took exactly the same route in the opposite direction, and working it on 8 April 1955 is No 149, at the junction of Newhaven Road and Ferry Road.** *David Clarke*

Metro-Cammell built two trams in 1933, Nos 260 and 265. They had flat corners to the platforms and Maley & Taunton trucks. These pictures show both trams in Newhaven Road on 8 April 1955. The van outside Rosebank Goods Station is a Fordson 5cwt. *Both David Clarke*

*Above:* **This is No 216 at St Andrew Square on 8 April 1955. Before the bus station was opened in April 1957, Scottish Motor Traction used the pavement around the gardens in St Andrew Square as its main city departure point. The coach to the left with the SMT diamond mid-bus is an ECW coach-bodied Bristol LS6G from a batch delivered in 1954.**
*David Clarke*

*Below:* **No 222 runs along York Place on the same day. Tollcross tram depot was a red sandstone building situated on the north side of West Tollcross and survived until the end of the trams; however, it was not used as a bus depot and was sold and demolished. The depot had an allocation of 68 trams and the routes worked were 6, 9, 18, 23, 24 and 27. A fire station now occupies the depot site.** *David Clarke*

*Above:* **At Braids on that same April day in 1955 are trams Nos 138 and 20. No 138 was built in 1933 and was originally numbered 29 until one of the Metro-Cammell steel-bodied cars was given that number in 1935. Route 16 was one of the last survivors of the tramway system, being withdrawn in mid-week on Wednesday 12 September 1956. The car on the right is a Rover P4, and I think the model is a 75 Mark II.** *David Clarke*

*Below:* **The last year of tram construction at Shrubhill was 1950, when six trams were completed, Nos 48 to 50, 169, 172 and 225.**

**These were therefore only six years old when the last tram ran on 16 November 1956. This is No 169 at Buckstone Terrace, also on 8 April 1955. The parked car is a Triumph Renown, which is strictly the name given to the Triumph's large saloon car made from 1949 to 1954 but is, in reality, part of a three-car series of 1800, 2000 and Renown models. Together with the Triumph Roadster they were the first vehicles to carry the Triumph badge following the company's takeover by the Standard Motor Company. A Triumph Renown Mark I cost £991 in 1950, and the Renown Limousine in 1952 cost £1,440.** *David Clarke*

*Above:* **This is tram No 247, with No 28 in the background, at Morningside Clock on 8 April 1955. The clock was presented to the people of Morningside in 1910. The ironwork pillar was supplied by Walter MacFarlance & Co of Glasgow and the clock mechanism was made by James Ritchie & Sons of Edinburgh. It was intended for passengers using Morningside railway station, which opened in 1884 and closed to passengers in 1962.** *David Clarke*

*Below:* **Route 23 was one of most heavily used routes in Edinburgh, although it touched Princes Street only at the junction of Hanover Street and The Mound. Electrification of the route was not completed until June 1924, and the extension to Morningside station was made in July 1929. At Morningside a siding was put into Belhaven Terrace to take the trams off a busy road. This is tram No 198 at Morningside terminus, also on 8 April 1955.** *David Clarke*

*Above:* **On that same day, working route 14 at Churchhill, is No 149. The nearest van is a Morris Minor, which was first introduced in 1952, making this particular vehicle less than three years old. The van in the distance is a Morris LD1, which was also available from 1952.** *David Clarke*

*Left:* **Later No 226 was photographed in Leven Street, being followed by an Orion-bodied Leyland PD2/20. The convertible heading in the opposite direction is an Austin A40 Somerset; one tested in 1953 had a top speed of 74mph and could accelerate from 0 to 60mph in 28.6 seconds. A fuel consumption of 30.1 miles per gallon was recorded, and the purchase price was £705.** *David Clarke*

*Above:* **At Tollcross on 8 April 1955 are trams Nos 173 (left) and 160. In the middle of the junction is the distinctive ironwork pillar clock that has been there since 1910. The lorry heading towards the camera is a Bedford O Series.** *David Clarke*

*Below:* **This view at Greenhill Gardens on the same day provides an interesting comparison between No 367, on the right, which was the first new car built at Shrubhill works to have a fully enclosed top deck, entering service in August 1929, and No 239, which was built in 1934 by Hurst Nelson with a domed roof and fitted with Maley & Taunton trucks.** *David Clarke*

*Above:* Twenty new all-metal trams were delivered during 1935, eight by Hurst Nelson and six each from English Electric and Metropolitan-Cammell. This is tram No 23, built by English Electric, at Grange Road on 8 April 1955 working route 13, the Churchill and Granton Circular. *David Clarke*

*Below:* Crossing the swing bridge on Commercial Street and Bernard Street on the same day is tram No 81. During 1935 to 1937 No 81 was the subject of experimental work on regeneration by Maley & Taunton, whereby the motors acted as generators while running downhill or stopping, the energy being returned to the overhead, which led to less pressure on the power station. There were difficulties, however, and the route used was to Levenhall. A total of 12 tramcars were altered, but by early 1939 the regenerative cars had been withdrawn and reverted to normal motor operations. *David Clarke*

*Above:* In the early days of electric traction route 19 had been between Morningside and Newington, but from July 1929 the number was vacant. In October 1935 route 19 became a new service between Tollcross and Seafield, extended to Craigentinny Avenue, with weekend workings to King's Road in April 1936. This is tram No 25, built by Metropolitan-Cammell in 1935, in Craigentinny Road, working route 19 on 8 April 1955. The railway line to the right is, I think, between Meadows Yard and South Leith. *David Clark*

*Below:* This excellent view of tram No 62 was taken in Dundas Street on 2 July 1956. *David Clarke*

*Above:* **This is tram No 45 in South St Andrew Street, also on 2 July 1956. The impressive building to the left of this view is the Prudential Assurance building, which was designed by Alfred Waterhouse and opened in 1895, and is now a grade B listed building.** *David Clarke*

*Below:* **Only two Standard trams were built at Shrubhill in 1941, Nos 72 and 211. Seen here** on the same day as the previous photograph is No 72 in St Andrew Square. Fifty AEC Regal 1s and Regal IIIs were lengthened to 30 feet and rebodied between 1952 to 1954 with Burlingham Seagull coach bodywork, and one of these attractive coaches can be seen in the background. The column on the left is the Melville Memorial, commemorating Henry Dundas, the first Viscount Melville. *David Clarke*

*Right:* **Turning from York Place into St Andrew Street on 2 July 1956 is tram No 32. The car heading in the opposite direction is a Morris Minor Series II, of which nearly 270,000 were built between 1952 and 1956. This model could reach the dizzy heights of 62mph flat out, 0 to 60 in 28.6 seconds, and cost £631 in 1952.** *David Clarke*

*Below:* **Seen on the same day are trams Nos 219, 214 and 222 in Broughton Street. No 219 was new in 1948, 214 in 1940, and 222, in the distance, in 1939. The van approaching the camera is a Trojan 1 tonner; by 1948 a completely new design for a medium-size van had been drawn up by Trojan with a conventional chassis and shaft drive through a normal gearbox. At first these vans used a modified version of the original engine design, which had been given two extra cylinders on the side of the block to act as injector pumps for the fuel. Though this method worked quite well, fuel consumption was rather heavy and a three-cylinder Perkins** diesel engine was substituted. This model was produced in various forms including personnel carriers, trucks, an articulated version as well as the normal and forward control 1 ton vans. I believe production of the Trojan ceased in 1959. Today it's the Dinky Toy models of the old Trojan vans that are likely to be of more interest to collectors, and possibly worth more than the full-size vans. *David Clarke*

*Above:* **This is tram No 73, one of only five Standards built by Shrubhill in 1947, at Picardy Place, also on 2 July 1956. The vehicle to the right of No 73 looks like a Rolls Royce hearse.** *David Clarke*

*Below:* **Tram No 47 was one of only two Standards completed by Shrubhill in 1946, and is seen in Elm Row on the same day.** *David Clarke*

*Above:* **Tram 212 was captured in Shrubhill Place on 2 July 1956.** *David Clarke*

*Below:* **In the earlier 1930s the Corporation authorised expenditure of £4,000 for a completely new, modern design of car. The body was built at Shrubhill and included a steel frame with timber infill; each side of both the lower and upper saloon was built as one piece, and the pillars extended from frame to roof. The roof was 'Masonite' covered with an** aluminium sheet. **The entrance was inset from the corner pillars, so that the folding step, when lowered, did not stick out. The tram was numbered 180 and was put on an EMB truck from No 177 with EMB air brakes. It weighed 13 tons complete, and entered service on route 12 on 3 April 1932. After a few days a Maley & Taunton truck and airbrake replaced the EMB equipment. No 180 is seen at Pilrig on the same July day.** *David Clarke*

*Above:* Towards the end of 1934 the prototype for the new standard design of tram was completed at Shrubhill. The design combined the best features of the various experimental trams and was, in my opinion, an attractive tram. A capacity of 62 seats was achieved by dispensing with upper-deck bulkheads and by widening the lower deck to take two seats abreast. The prototype, numbered 69, is seen passing Leith depot on 2 July 1956. Leith depot, situated near the Foot of Leith Walk, had two separate lines to the street from either side of the depot. It was refurbished in 1937 and converted to a bus garage in 1956, a purpose it still serves today. *David Clarke*

*Below:* This is No 235 on Leith Walk on the same day. In the background, working route 12, is a Metro-Cammell-bodied Daimler CVG6, new to Edinburgh in 1949. The bridge carried the former Caledonian Railway's Leith New Lines across Leith Walk en route to the eastern docks. This line opened in 1881 and was used almost exclusively for goods; the last section, at Leith East Yard, closed on 31 December 1973. In the background can be seen the clock tower of Leith Central station. *David Clarke*

At the foot of Leith Walk, also on 2 July 1956, is tram No 217. On the right is Leith Central railway station, which served as the terminus of a North British Railway branch from Edinburgh Waverley. The station was built on a large scale, including a train shed over the platforms. Until 1952 it had a regular passenger service to Edinburgh, a journey of just over a mile. The most striking feature of Leith Central was its size – it occupied a whole town block at the foot of Leith Walk, being bounded by Leith Walk on the western side, Easter Road on the east and Duke Street to the north. The four platforms were about 15 feet above street level, with the buffer stops at the western end. On this, the Leith Walk side, the station was entered by doors on the corner of Duke Street, leading to stairs up to the ticket office, waiting rooms and other passenger facilities, which were situated at platform level, one storey above the street. Below the platforms were retail premises on the Leith Walk and Duke Street sides of the Foot of the Walk, most notably the Central Bar, which still exists.

Following closure to passengers, the station was adapted to become a motive power depot for the new Swindon-built Inter City diesel multiple unit train sets used on express services, from 1956, between Edinburgh Waverley and Glasgow Queen Street. It was finally closed completely in 1972, and became derelict. The site of the station currently houses Leith Waterworld and a supermarket. The buildings that housed the station offices, waiting rooms, etc, the station clock and the shops at street level all still stand at the foot of Leith Walk. *David Clarke*

*Above:* **Approaching the camera at the junction of Leith Walk and Great Junction Street, is tram No 66, one of only two trams built new in 1946. The cinema on the corner is the Leith Palace, which opened in 1913 with around 2,000 seats. It closed as a cinema on 31 December 1966, and was then used for bingo. A Wetherspoon's pub now occupies the ground floor, while in the disused upper area the cinema seats, etc, are still intact, the stairs and swing doors to the balcony have survived in original 1966 decor, including the carpet, and the rear of the balcony has the original brown and gold panelling on the walls. The films featured on 2 July 1956 are *A Letter to Three Wives* with Linda Darnell and Kirk Douglas, and *Never Say Goodbye*, with Rock Hudson and David Janssen.** *David Clarke*

*Below:* **This is tram No 164 in Constitution Street on the same day. The street has an unusual claim to fame. On 9 January 1823 the last two men executed for piracy in Scotland were hanged at the north end, near what is now Tower Street. In the summer of 1822 Peter Heaman from Sweden and Francois Gautiez from France were found guilty of capturing the brig *Jane* en route from Gibraltar to Brazil, killing its master and stealing 38,000 Spanish dollars. The crowd witnessing the execution was said to be huge – 40,000 to 50,000 people.** *David Clarke*

*Above:* **No 145 is seen at Tollcross at almost exactly 10.00am on 3 July 1956. Note the police box with the air raid siren on top. The police box is still there, now moved just a few yards across the junction to stand next to the rather plain and dull Bank of Scotland offices on what was a gap site for years, behind** where Goldbergs used to be at Tollcross. I think the air raid siren was still on the police box until the 1960s. *David Clarke*

*Below:* **Tram No 217 is followed by 52 in Lothian Road on the same day.** *David Clarke*

*Above:* **This is No 169 followed by No 49 at the Usher Hall, also on 3 July 1956. Both trams were built in 1950 and were therefore only six years old when this photograph was taken. On the left is the former Caledonian Railway goods yards and the Caledonian Hotel, while the Usher Hall is just out of the picture on the right. The Caledonian Hotel, a grand railway hotel, was eventually built above the main entrance of the Caledonian's Princes Street station and opened, after some construction delays, in 1903. It was built in red sandstone from the west of Scotland. Princes Street station closed on 6 September 1965.** *David Clarke*

*Below:* **On North Bridge on the same day we see tram No 190, with the North British Hotel on the left. The car on the left is a Jaguar Mark VII, which was launched by Jaguar Cars at the 1950 London Motor Show. It was produced between 1951 and 1954 and had a 160bhp engine. The Mark VII VM was launched at the London Motor Show in October 1954 and had a 190bhp engine and a claimed top speed of 104mph. By the end of production a total of just under 31,000 of both versions had been were built, and if you had £1,693 in 1952 you could purchase one of these large four-door sedans.** *David Clarke*

*Right:* **This is Princes Street at the junction of Hanover Street on 3 July 1956, and traversing the junction is tram No 204. The lorry behind it is carrying Trebor sweets, made by Robertson & Woodcock, who opened a small factory in Shaftesbury Road, Forest Gate, London, in 1907. A larger, art deco building on the corner of Shaftesbury Road and Katherine Road was built in 1937. The company ceased making Trebor sweets in 1980 and the brand was purchased by Cadbury Schweppes. The car disappearing to the right is a Sunbeam Talbot 90, which was built between 1948 and 1954; 20,381 were produced, and in 1952 you could purchase one of these curvaceous cars for £1,393.** *David Clarke*

*Below:* **No 173 climbs Hanover Street on 3 July 1956. The building in the background with 'RSA' on the front is the Royal Scottish Academy, which has occupied William Henry Playfair's building since 1826. He was commissioned by the Institution for the Encouragement of Fine Arts in Scotland to design the building in 1822. Playfair died in Edinburgh in 1857 and is buried in Dean Cemetery in the city.** *David Clarke*

*Right:* **David Clarke then photographed No 56 crossing the junction of George Street with Hanover Street. The statue, made of bronze, is of King George IV. Sculpted by Sir Francis Chantry and funded by public subscription, it was erected in 1831 to commemorate the visit of the King to Edinburgh in 1822, the first Hanoverian monarch to visit Scotland; the visit was orchestrated by Sir Walter Scott. As a monarch, the King led a rich life; he was always in debt and relied on Parliament for financial help.** *David Clarke*

*Main picture:* **The next view taken that day shows the quite steep hill of Hanover Street at its junction with Queen Street. The tram is No 238.** *David Clarke*

*Right:* **In a similar position in Pitt Street on 3 July 1956 is tram No 173. I think the parked car might be a Riley tourer.** *David Clarke*

*Below:* **A total of five Standards were built at Shrubhill in 1938, and one of these was No 63, seen here at Brandon Street, also on 3 July 1956. The tram is working route 23, one of the best known and most heavily used routes of the Edinburgh system, although it only touched Princes Street where it crossed between Hanover Street and The Mound. Route 23 and the short-lived route 28 were the last to operate. The bus behind, judging by its lack of route number and blinds, is a brand-new Alexander-bodied Guy Arab IV being delivered from Falkirk.** *David Clarke*

*Right:* **In Inverleith Row on 3 April 1956 is No 229. Behind is a brand-new Alexander-bodied Guy Arab.** *David Clarke*

*Below:* **No 209, seen here at Goldenacre on 3 July 1956, had the distinction of being the only new tram built at Shrubhill during 1943. The van behind it is an early version of a Trojan.** *David Clarke*

*Above:* **In January 1954 route 16 was diverted to Bernard Street and reduced to part-day operation. From 17 June 1956, however, the route was extended to Granton to compensate for the withdrawal of routes 13 and 14. Seen at Granton on the same day as the previous picture while working route 16 is No 32; the tram behind is No 216.** *David Clarke*

*Below:* **No 216 has a problem at Granton on the same day, and is being attended by one of Edinburgh Corporation's three Austin tower wagons, EFS 743, DWS 528 and FSF 747.** *David Clarke*

*Above:* **No 83 is at Trinity Bridge, also on 3 July 1956. The Edinburgh, Leith & Newhaven Railway opened on 31 August 1842 between Scotland Street, in Edinburgh's New Town, and Trinity Crescent, near the Chain Pier. Granton Harbour opened in 1838 and the section from Trinity to Granton, which included Trinity Bridge, opened on 19 February 1846. The opening of the Forth Bridge in 1890 resulted in main-line trains to the north ceasing to use the Granton to Burntisland route, after which the Granton branch was used only for local passenger trains and goods traffic. The passenger trains stopped in 1925, a few years after the Edinburgh and Leith tramway systems were joined and passengers could travel into Edinburgh city centre without a** change of tram. Goods trains ran until 1986, after which the line was lifted. *David Clarke*

*Below:* **This is No 234 at Newhaven Pier Place on 3 July 1956. In the background is the lighthouse on Newhaven harbour wall, which was built in 1869. Newhaven was at one time a major oyster port and also played a role in the whaling industry.** *David Clarke*

*Above:* **A nearly deserted Annfield is seen on the same day, and approaching the camera is No 217.** *David Clarke*

*Below:* **Passing the bonded warehouse of Macdonald & Sons in Commercial Street, also on 3 July 1956, is No 72. At its peak there were around 100 warehouses in Leith storing wine and brandy. In the late 1880s, due to the collapse of the wine harvest in Europe, most of these were 'converted' to whisky storage.**

Around 85 bonded warehouses still stood in Leith in the 1960s, which between them matured around 90% of all Scotch whisky. One of the largest was Crabbies on Great Junction Street, which stored whisky for some of the foremost whisky distilleries, including Lagavulin, Talisker and Laphroaig. The last bond, on Water Street, closed around 1995. The Macdonald bonded store became a Grade B listed building in 1994. *David Clarke*

*Above:* **Picking up passengers at Loch Place on the same day is No 248.** *David Clarke*

*Below and following page:* **This is Bernard Street swing bridge on 3 July 1956, and crossing it in these two views are trams Nos** 210 and 32. **In the left background is the Old Ship Hotel and King's landing. Leith was the port of entry for the visit of King George IV to Scotland in 1822, and the Old Ship and King's landing was then given its new name to mark the event.** *Both David Clarke*

**The third view of the swing bridge shows No 216 followed by 219.**
*David Clarke*

*Top:* **This is No 180 on Constitution Street by the Police Office, also on 3 July 1956. Leith Town Hall, on the corner of Constitution Street and Queen Charlotte Street, was designed by R. & R. Dickson and built between 1827 and 1828. Following the amalgamation of Edinburgh and Leith in 1920, it was no longer required and became a police station. The wood-framed estate heading in the opposite direction is a Morris Minor Traveller, which was first available in 1952.** *David Clarke*

*Centre:* **Trams Nos 37, 165 and 210 are seen at the junction of Morningside Road and Colinton Road on 12 July 1956. This junction is called Holy Corner, as there is on each corner of the crossroads a church, although two are slightly set back – they are Christ Church, Morningside United and Morningside Baptist Church, and the fourth has been turned into the Eric Liddell Centre.** *David Clarke*

*Bottom:* **This is Morningside terminus on the same day, and the tram is No 217. Morningside cemetery, in the background, was opened in 1878, the first of a new generation of cemeteries built on the edge of the city. Nobel Prize-winning scientist Sir Edward Appleton is buried here; his prize was awarded to mark his contributions to the knowledge of the ionosphere, which led to the development of radar.** *David Clarke*

*Above:* **Trams 210 and 224 run along Comiston Road on 12 July 1956.** *David Clarke*

*Below:* **Route 11 reached the terminus at Fairmilehead on 19 April 1936. The intention** had been to build the line beyond this to Hillend, but the tracks never went beyond the north side of this busy road junction. No 72 is seen at Fairmilehead on the same day. *David Clarke*

*Right:* **The last Standard built at Shrubhill was No 225 in 1950, and it is seen here in Pentland Terrace on 12 July 1956. Edinburgh Corporation had chosen this tram for preservation, but just after this view was taken it was damaged beyond repair in a bus/tram collision.** *David Clarke*

*Below:* **On the same day No 173 is working route 23 at Tollcross. The first 60 trams sold in 1953, after the withdrawal of the Comely Bank, Stenhouse and Slateford routes, went for scrap to the Coatbridge firm of James N. Connell for £90 each; they were driven to Corstorphine terminus and winched aboard a low-loader, then, after the closure of that route, they were loaded at North Junction Street, then later still at Shrubhill.** *David Clarke*

At Tollcross, at the junction of Lauriston Place on 12 July 1956, No 236 awaits the go-ahead from the traffic policemen. The second picture, taken just after midday in Lauriston Place, shows No 238 and a gentleman who seems to have had a great urge to pass water...! *Both David Clarke*

*Above:* This is Lauriston Place again on 12 July 1956, and approaching the camera is No 234. The Glasgow-registered two-door roadster is, I think, an MG T-type Midget, production of which started in 1936 and, through various models, ended in 1955. This particular model is a TA, TB or TC. *David Clarke*

*Below:* The Lawnmarket is the general designation of that part of the town that is a continuation of the High Street, but lies between the head of the old West Bow and St Giles's Church, and is about 510 feet in length. In Lawnmarket on the same day is tram No 173. *David Clarke*

These two views were taken in Forrest Road on that same July day. Working route 23 is No 204, then a more distant view of No 219. The three-wheel van on the right of the second picture is a Reliant 5cwt, and the car on the left is a Skoda 440. *Both David Clarke*

*Above:* The Mound is an artificial hill in central Edinburgh that connects the New Town and Old Town and was formed by dumping around one and a half million cartloads of earth excavated from the foundations of the New Town into the drained Nor Loch, which forms today's Princes Street Gardens. The Mound was officially opened in 1781, and when the Edinburgh & Glasgow Railway was extended to Waverley station in 1846 tunnels were driven under The Mound to allow access to the west. Climbing The Mound on 12 July 1956 is No 137. *David Clarke*

*Below:* Some of Edinburgh's most notable buildings and institutions are found on The Mound, including the National Gallery of Scotland, the Royal Scottish Academy, the

spires of New College, the General Assembly Hall of the Church of Scotland, the headquarters of the Bank of Scotland and the Museum on The Mound. No 236 has just turned off Princes Street and is heading up the Mound, also on 12th July 1956. *David Clarke*

*Above:* **At the very busy junction of Princes Street, Hanover Street and The Mound is No 157. The bus working route 27 from Oxgangs Terrace to Crewe Toll is a Metro-Cammell Orion-bodied Leyland PD2/20. The car in the middle of the picture on the opposite side of Princes Street is a Triumph Mayflower, which was built between 1949 and 1953, during** which time 35,000 were produced. The 1952 car which had a three-speed gearbox with a column shift and a top speed of 62.9mph, and was yours for £505. In the same year the Morris Minor was priced at £384, and the Hillman Husky estate, behind the Triumph, £564. *David Clarke*

*Above:* **When this view of No 32 was taken on 12 July 1956 in Elm Row there were just four tram routes working. Two months later, on 12 September, tram routes 11 and 16 were replaced by buses.** *David Clarke*

*Below:* **Halted by the traffic policeman at the west end of Princes Street on the same day is tram No 45. The last day of tram operations was Friday 16 November 1956, and even though the Suez oil-supply crisis had begun there was no reprieve for the trams of Edinburgh. No 45 was still on fleet strength that day, and happily one tram was saved from the scrapyard, No 35.** *David Clarke*

*Above:* **In 1949 Edinburgh bought seven Bedford OBs to update its coach fleet. They had Duple Vista coach bodywork and the fleet numbers X2/9/18/22-25 (GWS 463 to 469). Together with a number of rebodied wartime Bedford OWBs, they were the backbone of the City Tours fleet until their withdrawal in 1958 and 1959. Originally in the madder and white livery, from 1955 a new black and white coach** livery was adopted. Standing at the City Tour bus stance on Waverley Bridge, looking very smart, is X22 (GWS 466). *Phil Sposito*

*Below:* **Also in 1949 the bulk of a large order for Daimler buses with Metro-Cammell Birmingham-style bodywork was delivered. This order comprised 10 CVD6s and 62 CVG6s, numbered 113 to 184, the first ten having Daimler engines. Working route 24 on Princes Street in the late summer of 1960 is No 163 (GSF 995). In the background is R. W. Forsyth, the ladies and gents outfitter. Forsyth was born in the Lothians but his first department store was in Glasgow. Following its success, in 1907 he opened a new store at 30 Princes Street designed by Sir John James Burnet, which was the first steel-framed building in Scotland. I believe it is now a Burton's store.** *Phil Sposito*

*Above:* **During 1952 Edinburgh Corporation purchased 16 all-Leyland Royal Tigers with rear-entrance bus bodywork, Nos 803 to 818 (HWS 768 to 783). They were initially used on the Comely Bank tram replacement, but soon transferred to other routes. Between 1957 and 1960 they were rebuilt at the Shrubhill works with front entrances; initially Nos 803 to 805 and 814 to 818 were coaches and the remainder buses, but later Nos 806 to 813 were also converted to coaches. The coaches were fitted with microphones and loudspeakers, and were finished in the black and white coach livery. This is No 818 (HWS 783) on Waverley Bridge in the summer of 1960. Nos 803 to 818 had all been withdrawn by 1966.** *Phil Sposito*

*Below:* **During 1955 Edinburgh Corporation took delivery of its second batch of 100 Metro-Cammell-bodied Leyland PD2/20s, Nos 501 to 600 (LWS 501 to 600). Working service 15 to Joppa in Princes Street in the summer of 1971 is No 526 (LWS 526).**

*Above:* **Working the former tram route 23 between Granton Road and Morningside is another of the batch, No 568 (LWS 568), seen crossing George Street in the winter of 1965. The interesting selection of cars and a van parked in the middle of George Street includes (from left to right) a Ford Zephyr 6 Mark III, either a Riley Elf or Wolseley Hornet, a Jaguar Mark II, a Morris Minor and a Ford Thames 300E van.** *transporttreasury.co.uk*

*Below:* **On North Bridge in the summer of 1972 is No 709 (NSF 709), a Metro-Cammell Orion-bodied Leyland PD2/20; new in 1956, it** was part of a batch of 100 delivered between 1956 and 1957. It is passing what was then the North British Hotel, known as the 'NB'. Resulting from a competition in 1895, the hotel opened in 1902. It was designed by architect W. Hamilton Beattie, and was a traditional railway hotel built for the railway company of the same name adjacent to its Waverley station. It kept the same name until the late 1980s, when, after refurbishment, it was renamed the Balmoral Hotel. Route 11 replaced tram route 11 working between Newhaven in the north and Fairmilehead, a suburb in the south-west of the city.

Between December 1961 and March 1962 the Corporation took delivery of 50 Alexander-bodied Leyland PD2A/30s, Nos 601 to 650 (YWS 601 to 650). Working route 22 on the east side of St Andrew Square is No 610 (YWS 610). All were initially allocated to Longstone garage to replaced elderly Guy Arabs. A feature of these buses was the illuminated advert on the offside panel, and they were the first batch of buses to come with interior fluorescent lighting. Route 22 was one of the Corporation's longest, going from Sighthill in the west, across the city to the port of Leith in the north, then westward to Granton and the suburb of Blackhall. It took buses 65 minutes between termini, and revenue returns for this popular route were among the highest! The 22 had effectively replaced tram routes 2 and 22, with considerable extensions at either end, at the western end from Stenhouse to Sighthill and at the northern end from Granton

to Blackhall. To maintain the 10-minute frequency, 14 buses were required from Leith and Longstone garages.

St Andrew Square is located at the east end of George Street. Its construction began in 1772, as the first part of the New Town, and it was designed by James Craig. Within six years of its completion the Square became one of the most desirable and fashionable residential areas in the city. As the 19th century came to a close, it evolved into the commercial centre of the city, and today residential housing is restricted to the northern side. Most of the rest of the Square is made up of major offices of banks and insurance companies, making it one of the major financial centres in Scotland; indeed, it claims to be the richest area of its size in the whole of Scotland.

*Above:* In 1959 36 pre-war Daimler single-deckers were still in regular service in the Corporation fleet, even though some dated back to 1932. Following trials, 50 new Weymann-bodied Leyland PSUC1/3s, Nos 1 to 50, entered service in 1959. A further 50 followed in 1960-61, and these seated 47, except for No 56, which had 45 seats plus luggage space at the front. Nos 51 to 55 and 57 to 62 were converted to one-person operation in 1961. Working route 13 in

Princes Street in June 1972 is No 52 (VSC 52). The bus behind is an Alexander-bodied Leyland PD3/6, new in 1964. If you were well off you went to Greens the hairdressers to get your hair done!

*Below:* Passing the entrance to Waverley station in June 1976 is another of the same batch, No 57 (VSC 57). The withdrawal of the 1960-61 batch of Tiger Cubs began in 1969, but some survived until 1978.

*Right:* In 1961 Edinburgh Corporation ordered a bus that was unique. It was a continental-style single-deck three-door bus with seats for 33 and standing room for a further 30. Legislation in 1961 permitted buses to be 36 feet long, and No 101 (YSG 101) was one of the first to this length. It first appeared at the 1961 Scottish Motor Show and entered service on route 16, a double-deck service, in April 1962. It was later transferred to single-deck route 1, then later to routes 45 and 46. In its original form it was not popular, and during 1969 it re-emerged as a one-door Airport service coach; it is seen in this role at Waverley Bridge in June 1972. By 1975 No 101 was back as a one-person bus and remained on fleet strength until April 1988.

*Below:* In January 1964 Edinburgh took delivery of six Duple-bodied Bedford VAL 14s, Nos 213 to 218 (213 to 218 SC), and seen here when brand new is No 214 (214 SC). The whole batch had a relatively short life in the Corporation fleet and all had been withdrawn by 1972. *Phil Sposito*

*Above:* Early in 1965 Edinburgh Corporation conducted trials with three double-deck demonstrators and its own Leyland PD3/6, No 684. The demonstrators were AEC Renown 7552 MX, Daimler Fleetline 565 CRW, and Leyland Atlantean KTD 551C. The outcome of the trials favoured the Fleetline and Atlantean, and 25 Alexander-bodied Leyland PDR1/1s were ordered. No 801 was delivered during 1965 and featured panoramic windows 7ft 11in long. The remainder of the batch, Nos 802 to 825 (EWS 802D to 825D) arrived during 1966, but only No 802 featured panoramic windows. Working route 37 on North Bridge is No 818 (EWS 818D). Sandwiched between it and another Alexander-bodied Leyland Atlantean is, I think, a Humber Sceptre, or perhaps a Singer Vogue. *transporttreasury.co.uk*

*Left:* The Leyland PDR1 with Alexander bodywork and panoramic windows became the standard bus for Edinburgh Corporation from 1967. Later a two-door, front-entrance and centre-exit layout was adopted, and the first deliveries of this layout arrived in 1969. They were Leyland PDR1A/1s with the fleet numbers 301 to 350 (PSC 301G to 350G), and working route 29 on Princes Street in the summer of 1972 is No 303 (PSC 303G).

*Above:* **From June to October 1970 Edinburgh took delivery of 50 Leyland PDR1A/1s with Alexander J-type bodies, but with the different frontal treatment from the previous batch. This wonderful view of No 380 (SSF 380H) at the east end of Princes Street at the junction of Waverley Bridge was taken in June 1972.**

*Below:* **Standing on Waverley Bridge in June 1972 is No 242 (VSC 242J), a Bedford YRQ with Duple bodywork that was new to Edinburgh Corporation in 1971. The Bedford Y series started production in 1970, and the YRQ was 10 metres long and had a Bedford six-cylinder diesel engine. The magnificent domed building in the background was, at the time of this view, the Bank of Scotland headquarters. The**

**bank bought the site on The Mound from Edinburgh Town Council in 1800 for £3,500 and the original building, designed by Robert Reid and Richard Crichton, was completed in August 1806 as a detached Georgian-style villa topped by a shallow saucer dome. In the 1850s the bank appointed David Bryce to extend and improve the building. He completely encased the original building and two full-height wings, crowned by domed lanterns, were added, and the central dome was replaced by a Florentine-style dome topped by a statue of victory by sculptor John Rhind. This transformation took place between 1864 and 1878 and the exterior has remained largely unaltered since.**